For Tamsin, J  Safiva

Contents

List of figures and tables

Figure

Tables

Acknowledgements

This book grew out of research undertaken for my PhD thesis which I started in 1999. I am grateful to everybody who helped me from that time, especially my supervisors, Dr Ray Hall and Professor Sarah Curtis (both then at Queen Mary), my sister, Kathryn Gray, and others who assisted me at the fieldwork stage of the PhD. I am very grateful to the young mothers who opened up their homes to me and spoke so candidly about their lives, and to the healthcare professionals who agreed to be interviewed and facilitated contact with potential respondents. Funding for the PhD research was provided by the Department of Geography, Queen Mary and the University of London Research Fund.

Thanks to my manager for many years at City University and then at the Institute of Education (University of London), Professor Helen Roberts, who helped me with my PhD, read journal papers arising from it and the outline for this book. I am indebted to her and to all my colleagues past and present, including Madeleine Stevens, Kristin Liabo, Dr Katherine Tyler and others from the Institute of Education, as well as colleagues at The Open University, especially Professor Rachel Thomson. Thanks also to Professor Philip Ryan (Carleton University), who gave me useful advice about constructionist perspectives on policy making. I am very grateful to the reviewers who read early drafts of the book and provided valuable feedback. Leila Ebrahimi at The Policy Press and Health and Society series editor Dr Mary Shaw have been supportive and patient throughout the writing of this book.

Abbreviations

ALSPAC	Avon Longitudinal Study of Parents and Children
ALSWH	Australian Longitudinal Study on Women's Health
BCS70	British Cohort Study 1970
BHPS	British Household Panel Survey
BMI	body mass index
CBS	Cardiff Births Survey
CHDS	Christchurch Health and Development Study
DCFS	Department for Children, Families and Schools
DCLG	Department for Communities and Local Government
DfES	Department for Education and Skills
DH	Department of Health
ECHP	European Community Household Panel
ECLS-K	Early Childhood Longitudinal Study (Kindergarten Class)
GHS	General Household Study
HOTN	Health of the Nation
LFS	Labour Force Survey
MUSP	Mater-University of Queensland Study of Pregnancy
NCDS	National Child Development Study
NLSAH	National Longitudinal Study of Adolescent Health
NLSY	National Longitudinal Survey of Youth
NRU	Neighbourhood Renewal Unit
ONS	Office of National Statistics
OR	odds ratio
PCT	Primary Care Trust
PSA	Public Service Agreement
SAGHS	South African General Household Survey
SES	socioeconomic status
SEU	Social Exclusion Unit
SSP	Sure Start Plus
TPS	Teenage Pregnancy Strategy
TPU	Teenage Pregnancy Unit

Part One
Making a problem

ONE

Introduction: 'shattered lives and blighted futures'

Teenage pregnancy as a problem

In the last decades of the 20th century successive British governments came to regard teenage pregnancy[1] as a significant public health and social problem. This view was shared, to varying degrees, by the governments of many developed nations, so that by the late 1990s eight of 28 OECD countries were actively intervening to reduce youthful conception and a further 12 countries considered teenage pregnancy to be a minor concern[2] (Unicef, 2001). In the UK, before and after the election of the New Labour government in 1997, teenage pregnancy was seen as a problem requiring intervention, and the British programme to address teenage pregnancy is an example of one of the more advanced and long-running initiatives of its kind in the developed world.

As a long-time commentator on this issue has observed, teenage pregnancy has become a 'veritable industry' (Furstenberg, 1991), but anxiety about youthful pregnancy is a comparatively new phenomenon. In previous eras, the age at which a woman began child bearing was not significant from a policy or any other perspective; the marital status of a mother-to-be was more important than her age. Marriage offered economic protection to mothers and their children in a time when the burden of unwed motherhood fell solely on local communities, so unmarried parenthood was highly stigmatised. At some point in the late 1960s/early 1970s, in the US (Arney and Bergen, 1984; Furstenberg, 1991; Wong, 1997), and slightly later in the UK (Selman, 1998/2001) and in other countries, such as South Africa (Macleod, 2003), public and policy concern shifted from the marital status of mothers-to-be to their age, and the problem of teenage pregnancy came into being.

There are a number of possible reasons why this shift in thinking occurred. The growing popularity of cohabitation among the middle (as well as the working) classes made unmarried child bearing a more difficult behaviour to condemn. The extension of adolescence, and the subsequent dependence of young people on their families for economic support, rendered youthful parenthood an increasingly problematic event. Longer, more convoluted transitions into education, employment and family formation – fuelled by structural changes in the economy, the need for increased participation in post-compulsory education and the rising costs of setting up an independent home – meant that early fertility increasingly came to be viewed as undesirable in that it would disrupt successful transitions to adulthood (Melhuish and Phoenix, 1987). Fertility among adolescents also came to upset deeply embedded beliefs about the innocence of childhood and the dangers of its corruption by premature sexual behaviour and reproduction (Fields, 2005).

A number of academic commentators have observed that the perception of teenage pregnancy as a problem in the latter half of the 20th century in the UK and elsewhere emerged as teenage fertility rates were starting their decline from highs in the middle decades of the century. Teenage pregnancy became a focus of policy concern in the US at an earlier stage than it did in the UK (Selman, 1998/2001): by 1975, anxiety about teenage pregnancy was entrenched in the US. And, in 1976, the Alan Guttmacher Institute (a US-based reproductive health organisation[3]) published its highly influential report *11 million teenagers: What can be done about the epidemic of adolescent pregnancies in the U.S.?* The publication of this report led to the widespread use of the word 'epidemic' in relation to teenage pregnancy and prompted further policy initiatives.[4]

In the UK, anxiety about teenage pregnancy occurred slightly later than in the US, reaching a peak in the late 1980s and early 1990s. Like the New Labour governments that followed them, Conservative governments (1979–97) considered early motherhood problematic, though this was often confused with anxiety about the rise of lone motherhood and politicians of the day made many inflammatory speeches about the role of 'single mothers' or 'young, lone mothers' in the erosion of civic values (Isaac, 1994; Daguerre, 2006). The Tories were sufficiently worried about teenage pregnancy to make its reduction one of the aims of their *Health of the Nation* (HOTN) initiative, which ran from 1992 to 1997. The HOTN target was to halve rates among 13- to 15-year-olds (from 9.6 to 4.8 per 1,000) by the year 2000 (Adler, 1997). This target was not reached and, when the New Labour government was elected in 1997, teenage pregnancy continued to be seen as a problem but was dealt with in an altogether different way.

'Teenage Pregnancy': the starting point

Teenage pregnancy was considered a problem before 1997 but the newly elected Labour government reinvigorated interest in the issue by making reductions in youthful conception rates a central focus of its efforts to tackle social exclusion: teenage motherhood was identified as a key consequence, and cause, of social exclusion. In 1999, the government published its seminal policy document on the issue entitled simply *Teenage Pregnancy* (SEU, 1999). The importance of this report should not be underestimated. It has been described as probably the 'single most influential recent document on the issue of teenage pregnancy in the UK' (van Loon, 2003, p 10). Entire sections of it appear, in only slightly modified form, at the front of the many local authority reports on teenage pregnancy. Much of the text has found its way into media coverage of teenage pregnancy, and *Teenage Pregnancy*'s analyses of the 'problem' as well as solutions to it are regularly referred to in the many scholarly articles on youthful reproductive and sexual health published since 1999.

Briefly, the report ran to some 139 pages, was organised into 11 chapters (with numerous appendices), and was replete with tables, graphs, charts, maps and other figures. The report's authors drew on a fairly large body of (mostly) public health and social science literature to describe the causes, correlates and consequences of teenage pregnancy, and to present the case for it being a significant social and public health problem and one, moreover, urgently in need of intervention. *Teenage Pregnancy* described the two government targets in relation to youthful pregnancy: the halving of conceptions among under-18s by the year 2010, with a downward trend in the under-16s rate to be established; and a reduction in the risk of teenage parents becoming 'socially excluded', to be achieved by increased (60%) participation in education, training or employment among young mothers. Both targets were to be met through the implementation of a highly coordinated, multifaceted national campaign known as the Teenage Pregnancy Strategy (TPS), which applied to England only; Wales, Scotland and Northern Ireland had to create and implement their own strategies.

Teenage Pregnancy was written under the aegis of the Social Exclusion Unit (SEU). The Teenage Pregnancy Unit (TPU), a cross-government unit, was later established to implement the TPS. Tony Blair, elected to power in a landslide victory just two years previously in 1997, provided the foreword to *Teenage Pregnancy* in which he memorably described youthful pregnancy as leading to 'shattered lives and blighted futures' (SEU, 1999, p 4). This bleak sentiment set the tone for *Teenage Pregnancy* and for New Labour's approach to youthful pregnancy and parenthood for the best part of the next decade.

Recent trends in teenage pregnancy: an overview

The publication of *Teenage Pregnancy* generated intense media interest in teenage sexual and reproductive behaviour. Before the election of New Labour in 1997 there had been a steady stream of articles in the British media about teenage sexual behaviour, pregnancy and motherhood. Some of this reported details of the previous Conservative government's attempts to tackle teenage pregnancy which, apart from HOTN, consisted largely of crass remarks about 'single, young mums' (Selman, 1998/2001; Daguerre, 2006). After the election of New Labour in 1997, coverage of teenage pregnancy slowly grew until 1999, when there was a substantial increase of reporting on the issue due almost entirely to the publication of *Teenage Pregnancy* and the creation of the TPS. *Teenage Pregnancy* also stimulated publication of papers in scholarly journals and other academic outputs.

What was lacking in much of the popular, and also some of the academic, coverage on teenage pregnancy was any meaningful description of trends in youthful conception. Much was made of comparatively high British teenage pregnancy rates compared with lower Western European rates, but there was little attention given to the *actual* rates of teenage pregnancy or changes across time. The increase in media coverage of teenage pregnancy that accompanied the introduction of the TPS was so intense that the general public could be forgiven for thinking that conceptions among young people were at an all-time high in the late 1990s. The *Sunday Mirror* referred to a 'baby boom' among teenagers and claimed that measures were needed to halt 'the upward spiral of teenage pregnancies' (news and leader, 13 June 1999, pp 2, 6). Even the usually less sensational broadsheets referred to a need to 'stem the tide of teenage pregnancies' (leader, *Independent*, 14 June 1999, p 3).

The scale of the 'problem' was described in detail in the first chapter of *Teenage Pregnancy* (SEU, 1999), where trends in early pregnancy and fertility in the UK were outlined. In the foreword, Tony Blair wrote that Britain had the 'worst record' on teenage pregnancies in Europe. And in the opening chapter the authors noted that in England 'there are nearly 90,000 conceptions a year to teenagers; around 7,700 to girls under 16 ... three-fifths of conceptions ... result in live births' (SEU, 1999, p 6). These observations, made at the beginning of the report, immediately invited the reader to see teenage pregnancy as a problem of some magnitude: the numbers quoted appear large. Yet, despite these ominous statements, and as noted briefly earlier and observed elsewhere (e.g. Duncan, 2007), there was a mismatch in timing between the release of *Teenage Pregnancy* and the highest incidence of teenage fertility (Table 1.1).[5]

Teenage fertility rates in England and Wales were highest in 1971, at nearly 51 per 1,000 women aged under 20, and after a steep decline in the 1970s showed only minor fluctuation in the following three decades (a range of 26.3–33 births per 1,000 females). By the beginning of the 21st century, fertility rates in women aged under 20 had almost halved, to around 29 per 1,000, compared with the 1971 rate. The more sustained recent decline in rates began in 2000, with falls in nearly every year from then on: the 2005 fertility rate was approximately 10% lower than the 2000 figure. In 2006, one in 15 of all births was to young women under 20 (approximately 45,000 births), constituting nearly 7% of all births (DCSF, 2008). Fertility rates show the proportion of pregnancies that end in birth. It may not have been teenage fertility that prompted the government to take action when it did, but rising teenage *pregnancy* rates. Table 1.2 shows teenage pregnancies from 1991 to 2005.

A similar trend to that seen in relation to fertility can be observed in rates of teenage pregnancy: the trend is (with some minor fluctuation) downward. As

Table 1.1: Teenage (under 20) fertility rates, England and Wales: various years, 1961–2005

Year	Rate
1961	37.3
1964	42.5
1966	47.7
1971	50.6
1976	32.2
1977	29.4
1981	28.1
1986	30.1
1991	33.0
1992	31.7
1993	30.9
1994	28.9
1995	28.5
1996	29.7
1997	30.2
1998	30.9
1999	30.9
2000	29.3
2001	28.0
2002	27.0
2003	26.8
2004	26.9
2005	26.3

Note: Rates are per 1,000 females aged under 20.

Source: Data taken from Table 3.1, *Population Trends 126* (ONS, 2006).

Table 1.2: Teenage (under 16, under 18, under 20) conception rates, England and Wales: various years, 1991–2005

Year	Under 16	Under 18	Under 20
1991	8.9	44.6	64.1
1996	9.5	46.3	63.2
1998	8.8	46.6	63.1
1999	8.2	44.8	62.5
2000	8.3	43.6	60.8
2001	8.0	42.5	60.3
2002	7.9	42.6	59.8
2003	7.9	42.1	60.3
2004	7.5	41.5	60.1
2005	7.8	41.1	59.0

Notes: 2005 data are provisional. Rates are per 1,000 females in relevant age range.

Source: Data taken from ONS (2007).

might be expected, conception rates are lower for the under-18s and lower still for under-16s, but the downward trend is broadly similar to that seen for all girls aged under 20. Examining rates of teenage pregnancy and fertility in this way, it is not evident why the New Labour government saw teenage pregnancy as a serious problem, one requiring intervention, when it did. The TPS was introduced in 1999 when under-20 fertility rates were nearly 31 per 1,000, or about 60% of the highest (1971) rate. Conception rates for under-20s, under-18s and under-16s were all lower than they had been in the previous year. There was no increase in these rates either before or around the time of the introduction of the TPS. It is possible that the UK's position on teenage pregnancy vis-à-vis other developed-world nations, described as the 'worst' in Europe in *Teenage Pregnancy*'s foreword, was the spur for the creation of the TPS. In this respect, justification for its introduction seems to be on firmer ground.

The overall trend in teenage child bearing in most developed nations is firmly downward – although there is wide diversity in the frequency of youthful pregnancy and its resolution. A Unicef Innocenti Report Card (No. 3) published in 2001, which attracted much press interest at the time, reported the latest available international data on teenage fertility in the developed world. This publication continues to be the most recent, authoritative, comparative analysis. In this report, the highest teenage fertility rates are described as being among US teenagers (with 52 births per 1,000 girls), and the lowest in Korea (2.9) and Japan (4.6). Although comparatively high at the time of the Unicef report, US teenage fertility rates were almost twice as high in the early 1960s, when there were nearly 90 births per 1,000 teenage girls (Singh and Darroch, 2000). And, despite diversity in youthful fertility rates, there is a clear 'Anglo-Saxon' domination of teenage pregnancy and fertility, with the US, Canada, Australia, the UK and New Zealand all experiencing higher rates of early pregnancy and child bearing than other developed nations (Chandola et al, 2001).

Three other issues relating to teenage sexual and reproductive behaviour are raised briefly here. First, the proportion of the teenage population engaging in sexual activity has increased over the last two decades, yet conception rates have not changed substantially, which suggests there is a trend toward increasingly effective use of contraception among youth (Wellings and Kane, 1999). Second, putting aside the issue of comparisons with other countries, not only are teenage pregnancy and fertility rates not rising, but they do not appear to be that high at all. Rates are expressed per 1,000 of the population at risk of experiencing the event. Consider these rates per 100 instead. Conception rates for girls aged under 16 in England and Wales in 2005 were about eight in 1,000, or *less than one in 100*. For 16- and 17-year-olds, the 2005 rate was 41 in every 1,000, or *four in 100*. In the same year, in a hypothetical group of 100 girls aged under 20, there will be, on average, fewer than *six pregnancies*. Fertility rates will be even lower, of course, because of the use of abortion. The scale of teenage pregnancy and child bearing is often overestimated, and more than one commentator has called for more 'perspective' in relation to our understanding of teenage pregnancy rates (Seamark, 1999).

Third, from the 1970s on, wider demographic changes, especially a decline in general fertility and changes in marriage, have profoundly affected the context within which child bearing at all ages, and certainly in the teenage years, occurs. The reduction in fertility among teenagers mirrors a decline in fertility among older women (which has been partly reversed by recent increases in the total fertility rate (TFR)).[6] Teenage fertility rates, as well as those in older women, started their descent at roughly the same time and in a similar way which suggests that there may be a relationship between the two groups. This is a reminder that it is not always helpful to see teenagers as a distinct population (Teitler, 2002).

However, it is in relation to marriage that the experience of teenage fertility has most changed over the last three or four decades. Three-quarters of births to teenagers were within marriage in 1971 (with conception often occurring outside it). By 2004, the proportion of teenagers who were married when they gave birth had fallen to 10%. The decline of marriage among adolescent mothers-to-be mirrors that seen in older age groups, although this decline has been steeper for teenagers. A teenage mother is now more likely, if she is 17 or older, to carry the baby to term and remain single or cohabit rather than marry. Or, if she is aged under 16, she is slightly more likely to end the pregnancy through use of legal abortion than she is to give birth.

Before the 1967 Abortion Act, teenagers resolved unplanned or unwanted pregnancies either by illegal abortion or by adoption. From the late 1960s on, pregnant young women were able to legally terminate their pregnancies. Although the UK has high teenage abortion rates (because it has relatively high teenage pregnancy rates), the ratio of teenage births to abortions is quite high compared with other countries, suggesting that pregnant teenagers often do not opt for termination of pregnancy even though this can be done legally and safely (Smith, 1993).

It is worth pointing out, in this brief overview of the recent historical context in which changes in child bearing have occurred, that teenage motherhood, viewed over a longer period, was not a historical commonplace (as is sometimes claimed by academic commentators questioning the problematisation of teenage pregnancy). Teenage child bearing was a rarity in Western Europe, as Hajnal showed in 1965 when he drew a line through the middle of Europe and described distinct Eastern and Western European marriage patterns, the former characterised by young age at marriage and near-universal marriage, the latter by higher age at marriage (age 24 for women, 26 for men) and relatively high (10%) rates of celibacy (Hajnal, 1965). Since fertility was largely confined to marriage, births to teenagers in Western Europe were unusual. These marriage patterns were linked to prevailing economic conditions: young people in Western European required adequate resources before marriage so remained single until they had secured them. Cook (2007) maintains that, in an English context, the relationship between income, ability to marry and age at marriage (and, therefore, fertility) shaped sexual and reproductive behaviour until the 1970s.

Rethinking teenage pregnancy as a problem

There is another issue that warrants discussion here in relation to the publication of *Teenage Pregnancy* in 1999, the creation of the TPS and the kind of policy and popular discussions about teenage pregnancy that were taking place at that time. Echoing the analysis presented in *Teenage Pregnancy* and most academic research and commentary, almost all of the coverage of the issue in the popular media depicted early child bearing as a negative phenomenon, the cause of ill-health, poverty and educational failure. The children of young mothers were also considered to be similarly fated to poor health and poverty and to repeat the cycle of disadvantage. The prime minister's foreword in *Teenage Pregnancy* was referred to for affirmation of this, as were the contents of the report itself. Teenage pregnancy came to be irrevocably associated with social exclusion – a belief widely accepted, and little interrogated, at the time.

Over the course of the next decade, as the TPS was being implemented and as there was a growth in research on teenage pregnancy, the relationship between youthful pregnancy and social exclusion came to the fore as part of a more general re-evaluation of the depiction of teenage pregnancy as a problem. Academic commentators argued, in particular, that the evidence that early fertility has deleterious outcomes is not as solid as once thought (and as starkly related in *Teenage Pregnancy*), and that young motherhood can be welcomed by teenagers, experienced positively and have benefits that are disregarded in conventional policy approaches (McDermott et al, 2004). The mismatch between the creation of the TPS and fertility rates among teenagers was also flagged up more prominently (Lawlor and Shaw, 2004), and there was greater examination of the meanings attached to teenage pregnancy and some exploration of the ways in which it has been constructed as a problem in the policy and academic literature (Cherrington and Breheny, 2005; Fallon, 2006).

It is impossible to know to what extent, if at all, this re-evaluation of teenage pregnancy has affected policy makers' perspectives and the policy-making process and its outputs, but the TPS is not as prolific as it once was and nothing else published by the TPU or other government departments on the issue of youthful reproduction has had the same impact as *Teenage Pregnancy*. Media coverage of teenage pregnancy has also declined. Towards the end of the first decade of the new century, teenage pregnancy's position as one of society's most pressing problems appears to have been eclipsed by the emergence of a new set of problems involving young people, such as knife crime or teenage suicide.

This re-evaluation of teenage pregnancy has occurred for a number of reasons but may be related to growing concern about the consequences of deferment of child bearing, including the possibility of a greater incidence of involuntary childlessness (Simpson, 2006). The perils of 'elderly' fertility have become a staple of the media, and the anomalous situation whereby teenage pregnancy is considered problematic but child bearing among women in their late 30s and 40s is not, even though the latter poses greater medical risks, has been described by academic commentators (Lawlor and Shaw, 2002; Benzies et al, 2006). Reconsideration of teenage pregnancy as a problem may also be related to a realisation that the TPS is unlikely to meet all its targets. Teenage pregnancy has declined in many English areas, but not as much as that needed if the TPS's 10-year targets are to be met. The TPU maintains that area variation in decreases is attributable to problems with the implementation of the TPS and not with the TPS itself (Amu and Appiah, 2006; DfES, 2006; Galavotti and Green, 2006), although the failure of the TPS targets on reduction of conception rates will likely force a reconsideration of the strategy itself.

The making and unmaking of a problem

The title of this book is *Teenage pregnancy: The making and unmaking of a problem*, but this is probably overstating the extent of the re-evaluation of teenage pregnancy, and it would be wrong to imply that this is what happened in the decade from the late 1990s on. Teenage pregnancy continues to be seen as a problem in academic and policy outputs and public discourse, and the TPS is still in place and may remain so beyond 2010. Moreover, the kind of re-evaluation of teenage pregnancy that has been taking place in the UK since the TPS came into being is not new: scholarly work questioning the depiction of teenage pregnancy as a problem dates from before the late 1990s (see, for example, Murcott, 1980), and a similar process of the problematisation and subsequent re-evaluation of teenage pregnancy occurred in the US several years before it did in the UK. Furstenberg (1991), speaking from a US perspective, points out that teenage pregnancy first emerged as a problem in the late 1960s and was firmly on the policy agenda within five or so years. Yet, within the next 10–15 years a number of 'revisionist' scholars questioned the problematic basis of teenage pregnancy and policy towards it. Furstenberg observes that:

> These doubts have emerged from different quarters but the skeptics share a common perspective: The issue has been misconstrued by careless and sometimes biased research, and it has been exaggerated and distorted by misguided reformers ... These commentaries ... have provoked disbelief and outrage by scholars in the field who have replied that the critics, not they, have distorted the facts ... But coming as they do from serious researchers, the

revisionist views cannot be easily dismissed. They demand that academics reexamine their assumptions and their evidence about how the timing of parenthood is linked to social and economic disadvantage. And, they compel policymakers to ask whether they are shooting at the right target. (p 127)

Furstenberg points to the (alleged) role of 'misguided reformers' as instrumental in bringing teenage pregnancy to the policy-making table. Evans (2006), from a British perspective and in a more general consideration of sexual health initiatives, makes a similar point. He describes the emergence of a 'sexual health policy community' in the 1980s that 'struggled to win policy attention and resources' (p 248).

Furstenberg briefly refers to Downs' (1972) influential work on public and policy responses to social problems, the 'issue–attention cycle'. This provides a convenient way of theorising the rise and decline of social problems like teenage pregnancy.

The cycle, Downs suggests, starts with a 'pre-problem' stage, where the 'problem' has not yet been widely recognised as such (though some interest groups may have already taken an interest in it and started to lobby policy makers). Downs observes that conditions regarding the problem are worse in the pre-problem stage than they are once the public becomes interested in the problem. Once recognition of a problem occurs, this causes 'alarm and euphoric enthusiasm', with the public clamouring for a solution. There is usually strong pressure from the public for political leaders to 'do something' about a social problem, though this is usually demanded with public resistance to the introduction of the kind of profound social changes that might alleviate the problem. Once it becomes obvious that simple solutions cannot be found ('realising the cost of significant progress'), the next stage of the cycle is one of declining interest, and the cycle ends with a post-problem stage, when the issue lingers in 'a twilight realm of lesser attention or spasmodic recurrences of interest'.[7] However, even though the problem has ceased to be seen as an urgent issue, the relationship between the problem and public attention to it is now different from what it had been in the first stage of the cycle. During the time that an issue is a problem, new institutions, programmes and policies will have been created to solve the problem and these remain in place, maybe in reduced or altered form, even though public attention may have moved elsewhere. Therefore, problems that have gone through the cycle usually receive a greater degree of attention than those still at the pre-problem stage.

Downs' work is now dated, but is a reminder that what passes for a social problem is time- and place-specific and dependent on the fulfilment of a number of conditions: that an issue will be considered sufficiently serious to be brought to the attention of a wider audience; that lobbyists are able to effectively petition for action to solve the problem; that policy makers will feel spurred into action by the existence of a particular social problem, for example.

Considering the British experience of youthful pregnancy from an issue–attention cycle perspective suggests that teenage pregnancy as a problem (and not just a social issue) appears to have passed through the cycle more rapidly than it did in the US. Nearing the end of the first decade in the 21st century, teenage pregnancy as a problem is probably in the fourth or even the fifth stage of the cycle, with declining concern as it is increasingly recognised that the problem cannot be properly dealt with (ie rates are not coming down as quickly as needed; policy and public attention has started to shift elsewhere) and 'spasmodic' recurrences of interest (from the media, minor policy initiatives). The latter implies, of course, that concern about teenage pregnancy is unlikely to go away and will be a feature of British society for some time. Even if it passes through a full issue–attention cycle (or even through several cycles), teenage pregnancy is always likely to be considered a problem in a world where fertility is increasingly deferred, education and training is prolonged and economic independence is lauded. Yet, however they are likely to be regarded in the near and distant future, there can be few examples of a population that has been as scrutinised as pregnant teenagers and teenage mothers. Teenage pregnancy has been (and continues to be) the site of starkly competing interests, with commentators from the religious, 'family values' Right through to the 'liberal' Left expressing concern about it. And, while teenage pregnancy as a problem pre-dates the New Labour government, *Teenage Pregnancy* and the TPS represent a significant turning point, at least in relation to the presentation of teenage pregnancy as a problem. It is the true starting point of this book.

Aim

The aim here is to consider the depiction of teenage pregnancy as a social and public health problem and to explore ways in which policy makers, academics and the media have responded to teenage pregnancy. The focus is on the late 1990s to the present, although the analysis is not confined to this period. The book largely covers the British (more specifically the English) experience, though reference is made to other countries' experiences of teenage pregnancy.

Parts and chapters

The book is written in two parts. In this, the first part (Making a problem), the focus is on describing the background to, factors associated with, everyday representations of and policy on teenage pregnancy. In the second part (Unmaking a problem), the depiction of teenage pregnancy as a problem is interrogated through an examination of the consequences of early motherhood, its presentation as a 'decontextualised' problem and an exploration of the reasons why teenage pregnancy emerged as a problem when it did, and what (if anything) its depiction as a problem means.

After this Introduction, there are six chapters and a conclusion. Chapter Two (Who has a baby as a teenager?) is descriptive and outlines the structural, demographic and psycho-social factors associated with teenage pregnancy and fertility. Reflecting the focus of the book, the chapter is centred on teenage women, but there is a brief section on teenage mothers' (male) partners, and also on young people who have been in the care system. In Chapter Three (Epidemics, fluctuations and trends: the everyday depiction of teenage pregnancy), after a brief section on the uses of demographic and other data, the representation of teenage pregnancy in the media is explored, focusing especially on the sensational language and other journalistic devices used to describe teenage pregnancy and young mothers. In Chapter Four (New Labour, a new approach to teenage pregnancy) the TPS, and *Teenage Pregnancy*, described briefly in the Introduction, are considered more fully. There are three reasons advanced in *Teenage Pregnancy* for youthful conceptions: structural ('low expectations'), technical/educational ('ignorance' about contraception and the reality of parenthood) and social or cultural ('mixed messages' about sex and parenthood). These and other features of *Teenage Pregnancy* will be discussed.

The consequences of early fertility are usually described as being medical/health-related or social (including socioeconomic) in nature, and are considered to affect teenage mothers and their children. Chapter Five (What are the consequences of teenage fertility?) aims to describe the literature on the effects of early fertility and summarise its main findings. In Chapter Six (Contextualising teenage pregnancy) it is argued that teenage pregnancy in the UK has been decontextualised as an issue by, among other things, the use of sometimes inappropriate international comparisons and a lack of understanding about the relationship between early conception and aspects of the British demographic, social and economic landscape. Teenage motherhood as a normative, and even positive, experience is also considered in Chapter Six. Chapter Seven (Theorising teenage pregnancy as a problem) is the most speculative chapter in the book and explores social-constructionist and related approaches to teenage pregnancy. With a focus on two political periods – the Conservatives in power from the 1980s to the late 1990s and the New Labour governments from the late 1990s onwards – the chapter considers how policy and wider social attitudes to pregnant and parenting teenagers are informed by the social conditions, norms and anxieties of the day.

Notes

[1] Important note on the use of terminology: the term 'teenage pregnancy' no longer refers just to adolescent conception: it has a wider meaning and is used to describe pregnancy and fertility and, to some extent, sexual behaviour among teenagers. 'Teenage pregnancy' has been used in this way here, though it is recognised that sex, pregnancy and fertility are all quite distinct phenomena. In demography, 'fertility' refers to the number of live births that a woman has. It is used synonymously here with 'child bearing' and 'motherhood,' primarily for stylistic purposes.

[2] In the data presented in the Unicef (2001) report there is no observable relationship between national concern about teenage pregnancy and the teenage fertility rate itself. For example, the Slovak Republic's 1998 teenage fertility rate was approximately the same as the UK's, but teenage pregnancy was not considered to be a problem in that country.

[3] The Alan Guttmacher Institute is now called Guttmacher Institute.

[4] It should be noted that the '11 million' in the title refers not to the number of pregnancies at that time, but the number of teenagers in the US population.

[5] In the UK, the Office for National Statistics (ONS) is the government department with responsibility for collecting and publishing official statistics about the UK's population and aspects of its society and economy. Conception, fertility and abortion data are collected, or derived, from vital statistics. Coverage of these events is likely to be near complete (it is a criminal offence to conceal a birth under the

1861 Offences against the Person Act, as is failure to register a child's birth within 42 days in England and Wales and 21 days in Scotland). Collection of data on use of abortion is mandatory and is governed by the 1967 Abortion Act. At present, there is no way to measure pregnancy using vital statistics. Conception rates are derived from summing births (including stillbirths) and abortions, which means that spontaneous abortions (commonly known as 'miscarriages') are excluded from calculations. Rates are constructed by dividing the total number of events (conceptions, births, abortions) by the population 'at risk'. So, for the construction of the under-20s' conception rate, the number of conceptions in this group is divided by the female population aged 13–19. The figure is then expressed as a rate per 1,000. Data are not available for conceptions to girls aged under 13 years. Conception rates are approximately one year behind, since data on births are needed to construct them. Further information about the collection of data and construction of rates is available in the TPU's *Teenage Pregnancy Data and Analysis Toolkit* (TPU, 2005), and in the 'Notes on data' section in ONS's *Conception Statistics* (ONS, 2005).

[6] The TFR is the average number of children born to a woman over her lifetime. It is calculated using age-specific fertility rates and is a 'synthetic' measure (Dharmalingam, 2004).

[7] www.anthonydowns.com/upanddown.htm

TWO

Who has a baby as a teenager?

Introduction

In the UK, public perceptions about the kinds of women who experience pregnancy and motherhood in their adolescence often combine elements of truth (that youthful pregnancy is more common among working-class teenagers, for example) and also aspects of the worst prejudices (that young women connive to become pregnant solely to claim welfare benefits and social housing). In contemporary British society, negative stereotypes about young mothers dominate the popular imagination and teenage mothers are generally considered to be young women deficient in morals and conduct, and even appearance. These popular ideas are not peripheral in young mothers' lives, as evidenced by the observation made by one practitioner running an 'image-based initiative' aimed at boosting the self-esteem of teenage mothers that '[young mothers] are aware of the Vicki Pollard[1] negative press that all teenager mothers are the same and they wanted to put across a different image' (Henry, 2005).

There is a large research literature on the factors associated with teenage pregnancy and motherhood in nations of the developed world, and it demonstrates that teenage pregnancy is not equally distributed in most populations. In addition to the widely acknowledged association of youthful conception and child bearing with relative poverty, teenage pregnancy can also be seen to have a distinct geography, to be a feature of certain family structures and, in some cases, to be associated with adverse childhood experiences, such as being looked after in the care system[2] or childhood neglect and abuse. An exploration of these and other factors is the focus of this chapter.

Some caveats

Before the literature is described further, three caveats should be briefly made. First – despite broad patterns that can be discerned in relation to teenage pregnancy, such as its being clustered in certain geographic locations or more prevalent among girls with poorer educational attainment, for example – there is inevitable variety among young women who become pregnant as teenagers. Teenage mothers hail primarily from working-class backgrounds, but not exclusively so. Occasionally, a girl from a middle-class family has a child as a teenager (and many more become pregnant but elect for abortion). It is statistically rarer, but not unknown. Similarly, there is variety in outcomes among individuals from similar backgrounds. Being poor or disengaged from the education system, for example, does not destine a young woman to teenage pregnancy: poverty and lack of engagement with education are *associated* with youthful conception, but do not lead inexorably to it. Hoffman (1998) reminds us that:

> Teenage mothers are individuals, so they naturally vary in their circumstances, their behavior and their well-being. (For example, they may be 14-year-olds still in junior high school or 19-year-old high school graduates.) And some of them end up doing rather well…. Consequently, there can be no 'one size fits all' conclusion here. (p 236)

Second, the factors associated with teenage *pregnancy* are not necessarily the same as those associated with teenage *fertility*. In analyses of teenage pregnancy it is common to confuse the two terms (this has been done throughout this book to reflect the way the phrase 'teenage pregnancy' is commonly used), but in this chapter the distinction between these two outcomes is important. Factors associated with *sexual behaviour* may also be different (Buhi and Goodson, 2007) but the focus here is on pregnancy and child bearing and not on sexual behaviour (though this is often examined in the research literature alongside pregnancy and fertility).

Third, the focus of this chapter is on relatively recent research (that is, from the late 1990s to the present) and, because of this, little can said about the ways in which late 20th-century/early 21st-century teenage mothers differ from teenage mothers of previous eras. Certainly, contemporary young mothers are less likely to be married than were teenage mothers in previous decades (though they may be in a cohabiting relationship). Inter-cohort analysis of British datasets (the 1958 and 1970 cohorts) has shown that family formation is becoming more diverse and complicated, and that the timing of parenthood is increasingly affected by entry into education (Berrington, 2003; Simpson, 2006). However, much work remains to be done on understanding longer-term changes in family formation behaviour and the timing of entry into parenthood, and how these interact with transitions into education and work.

There are a number of useful reviews of the literature on the factors associated with teenage pregnancy, the findings of which are used here. The most recent of these is the EU–wide Reprostat 2 study, a systematic review of factors operating at the level of the individual (that is, not macro-level factors) associated with teenage pregnancy (not fertility), one arm of which is based at the University of Aberdeen, in the UK (Temmerman et al, 2006; Imamura et al, 2007). Reprostat 2 examined quantitative studies only. Here, qualitative research studies are also drawn on, and research from the US and other developed nations is used (though the focus is primarily on British research). In the Reprostat 2 study, factors associated with teenage pregnancy were categorised into six broad groups (sociodemographic; family structure and stability; educational; risky health behaviours; sexual health knowledge, attitudes and behaviour; and service accessibility and acceptability). Here, for simplicity's sake, factors have been categorised into: *structural* (socioeconomic status; educational attainment and engagement with education; housing tenure; geographic location); *demographic* (ethnicity; family-of-origin status and other family factors); and *psycho-social* (risk taking and self-esteem; preference for being a young mother).

It would be impossible to cover the literature as widely as the Reprostat 2 study did (where 4,444 studies were initially screened). The aim here is to provide an overview of the research literature on the *key* factors associated with early pregnancy and fertility which will provide the reader with some background knowledge and put the following chapters into context. After a description of the factors associated with teenage pregnancy and fertility there is a brief section on the male partners of teenage mothers and the experience of pregnancy among young people who have been in the care system – groups traditionally overlooked in the literature on teenage pregnancy.

Factors associated with teenage pregnancy and fertility

Structural

The correlate of early pregnancy and motherhood referred to most frequently in the research literature from the developed world is socioeconomic status (SES). Compared with more affluent counterparts, young women from deprived, or relatively deprived, backgrounds are not only more likely to become pregnant but they are also more likely to carry the pregnancy to term (Garlick et al, 1993; Kiernan, 1997; NHS CRD, 1997; Rosato, 1999; Wellings et al, 1999; Darroch et al,

2001; McCulloch, 2001; Bonell et al, 2003; Coleman and Cater, 2006; Harden et al, 2006; Allen et al, 2007).

In the UK, women who have children in their teenage years are predominantly from social classes IV and V (Rosato, 1999). Young women from other social classes do become pregnant (though on a lesser scale than their working-class counterparts), but opt instead for termination. In Smith's (1993) analysis of pregnancy and abortion in Tayside, the highest teenage pregnancy rates were found in the poorest areas. Among girls aged less than 16 years, rates were three times higher than for those in the least-deprived areas. For girls aged 15–19 these rates were around five times higher in the period 1989–90. Teenage conceptions in the least-deprived areas were much more likely to be resolved by abortion: over 60% of teenage pregnancies in the least-deprived areas were terminated, compared with around half that figure in poor areas. Analysis of more recent data collected during the implementation of a sex education trial in England demonstrated that low SES (as measured by housing tenure) was significantly associated with teenage pregnancy (Bonell et al, 2003; Allen et al, 2007).

The relationship between SES and pregnancy and parenthood is evident in a British and other settings. In an Alan Guttmacher Institute comparative study (Darroch et al, 2001), stark differences between women in the five countries studied in relation to early child bearing by SES were observed. There was a clear gradient in the case of the UK, with higher proportions of women from lower SES groups bearing children in adolescence. Higher overall teenage fertility rates were found in the US, reflecting the fact that the US has the highest rates of teenage pregnancy in the developed world (Unicef, 2001), and there was evidence of strong differentials in sexual activity by race and by SES (see also Cheesbrough et al, 2002). In the Netherlands, where teenage fertility is rare, early parenthood is concentrated in the poorest (usually minority ethnic) groups (van Enk and Gorissen, 2000; van Loon, 2003). This is also the case in Sweden (Singh et al, 2001) and Spain (Nebot et al, 1997). In New South Wales, Australia, teenage mothers constitute about 2% of all women giving birth in the least-deprived areas and nearly 7% in the most deprived (Public Health Division, New South Wales, 2000).

The link between poverty and early pregnancy is well described, but much less understood, and many aspects of the relationship require further examination. Is it membership of social classes IV and V throughout childhood that is associated with teenage pregnancy, or being poor only in the teenage years? Is there a 'dose–response' relationship between poverty and reproductive outcomes? The fact that there is a gradient in teenage motherhood according to SES, with those in social class V approximately 10 times more likely to experience it than women in social class I (Botting et al, 1998), points to this possibility. There may be something about the experience of living in a pervasively poor environment on a long-term basis that affects reproductive outcomes. In one analysis of National Child Development Study (NCDS) data, 17% of teenage mothers reported financial hardship in their family of origin at age 7, as compared with 6% of women who had children at older ages; and 22% of teenage mothers reported hardship at age 16, as compared with 8% of older mothers. In multivariate analysis, girls who reported hardship at *both* points in time were nearly three times more likely to become young mothers than those who reported no financial hardship (Kiernan, 1997).

The behavioural or other mechanisms linking low SES to teenage pregnancy and child bearing are imperfectly understood. SES is confounded with myriad factors in a British setting: residence in social housing; educational opportunities and attainment; geographic location; access to health and other services. These can all, theoretically, affect reproductive behaviour, which makes the isolation of the effect of SES on outcomes methodologically difficult.

Teenage pregnancy and motherhood is strongly associated with poor educational attainment and/or a lack of engagement with education (that is, not liking being in school). Kiernan's (1997) analysis of NCDS data explored the relationship between childhood educational attainment and later child bearing. Teenage mothers were much more likely to have lower educational attainment scores at ages 7 and 16 than older mothers (44% of teenage mothers reported being in the lowest quartile for educational attainment at age 7, compared with 24% of older mothers). Differences for men and women were demonstrated, suggesting that educational achievement may be a more powerful deterrent to young motherhood than to fatherhood. In multivariate analysis, education continued to be significant and young women who experienced a decline in educational achievement over time were particularly likely to become teenage mothers. Educational achievement was cited as the most important factor in relation to early parenthood in the analysis.

A review of the relationship between SES, educational attainment and teenage sexual activity, pregnancy and child bearing undertaken in five countries (the UK, the US, Sweden, France and Canada) (Darroch et al, 2001) showed that, among women with low educational attainment, about 20% of Swedish women, 18% of French women,

45% of Canadian, 36% of British and 66% of US women became young mothers.

In the latter study, the data do not indicate whether low educational attainment preceded or was a consequence of child bearing. In the popular imagination, early parenthood is seen as a cause of school drop-out (SEU, 1999; Hosie, 2007), though many young mothers drop out of education *before* pregnancy and there may be a history of bullying that precedes this (Arai, 2004). In a Brazilian study (Heilborn et al, 2007), 40% of girls experiencing pregnancy in adolescence had already dropped out of school. In recognition of the poor educational attainment among teenage mothers, one of the Teenage Pregnancy Strategy's (TPS) aims is the greater inclusion of teenage mothers in the education system, and initiatives have been set up to achieve this (Dawson et al, 2005).

It is not just educational attainment that is important; attitudes to school and engagement with the education system also matter. A strong association exists between teenage pregnancy and the latter. In Arai's (2004) analysis of qualitative data collected from English teenage mothers, most of the young women interviewed had low educational attainment, many were disengaged from the educational system before pregnancy and some had been truants (more than one respondent was expelled from school) (see also, Bonell et al, 2005). In a study of engagement with the educational system among 93 teenage mothers in 10 English areas, lack of engagement was found to have intensified at secondary level and was accompanied by bullying and poor teacher attitudes to students. Despite these early negative experiences of school, many of the teenage mother interviewees expressed a desire to re-engage with education, which the author believes demonstrates that 'with the right support, pregnancy can present a golden opportunity to re-engage young women who have become disengaged pre-pregnancy' (Hosie, 2007, p 343).

In the UK, housing tenure (owner-occupation, private renting, renting from a local authority or housing association) is strongly confounded with SES and is often used as a proxy for income or SES (Bonell et al, 2003). A distinction should be made between a young woman's housing tenure *before* pregnancy and her experience *after* birth, though this may be the same. Botting and colleagues (1998) found that 80% of single mothers aged under 18 lived in someone else's (probably the parental) household in 1996–97. By age 18 or 19, this figure had decreased to 29%, with many of these young, lone parents moving into social housing. In Allen and colleagues' (2007) analysis of data collected from teenagers during a sex education trial in England, living in non-privately owned housing was significantly associated with increased risk of pregnancy at or before age 16 years. Bivariate analysis of data collected during another sex education intervention (in Scotland) showed similar results, with girls living in council or rented accommodation twice as likely to become pregnant as girls living in privately owned property (Buston et al, 2007).

It is widely believed that young girls become pregnant to secure welfare benefits and council housing (the latter a relatively scarce commodity in some parts of the UK). To date, there is no British research showing that young women knowingly become pregnant to gain access to social housing or other benefits. The young women in Allen and Bourke Dowling's (1998) study appeared naive about welfare benefits and the possibility of being granted a council property, and a report by the National Council for One Parent Families (2000) concluded that the housing needs of young lone mothers are often neglected and that young women are not given preferential treatment because of their age.

Given the kind of links between SES and housing tenure described above, it is not surprising that teenage pregnancy and fertility is concentrated in certain geographic (usually deprived) locations (SEU, 1999). Geographic variation in teenage pregnancy is central to the implementation of the TPS. As an area-based initiative, the TPS set area targets for the reduction of teenage pregnancy. These varied according to the existing level of teenage pregnancy in the area and, even in those places where teenage pregnancy rates were low there was a requirement to further reduce them. Richmond, for example, had among the lowest under-18 conception rates in London in the first years of the implementation of the TPS, yet was expected to take steps to further reduce rates (Richmond and Twickenham Primary Care Trust, 2002). In Lambeth, which had high under-18 conception rates, the target was a 60% reduction by the year 2010 (London Borough of Lambeth, 2001).

The Neighbourhood Renewal Unit (NRU, 2002), which worked closely with the Teenage Pregnancy Unit (TPU) in its early days, has described geographical variations in under-18 conception rates. In 2000, these ranged from 19.4 per 1,000 in Richmond upon Thames to 89.8 in Hackney: almost a five-fold variation. The Unit also described the *concentration* of teenage conceptions: between 1992 and 1997, more than half (54%) of all under-18 conceptions occurred in the 20% most-deprived wards. (This means, of course, that close on half of all conceptions to under-18s occurred at that time in less-deprived areas of England, a point often forgotten in the research describing the geography of teenage pregnancy).

Geographic analyses of teenage pregnancy and fertility in the UK and elsewhere fall (broadly) into two groups. First, there are simple mapping studies which do not attempt to significantly explore reasons for variation in rates but simply describe differentials by geographic area (the 'area' can be the region, the local authority or the ward). Authors sometimes use data on area-specific deprivation to link teenage pregnancy to SES. Analyses of the (relatively) simple kind include those undertaken by Smith (1993) and Garlick et al (1993). Both are now out of date but (in the case of the former, especially) are still regularly cited. In Smith's analysis of teenage conception in Tayside, rates in poor areas were three times higher than those in wealthier areas but pregnant teenagers in these areas were less likely to have abortions than pregnant girls living in more affluent areas. Since all abortions were carried out in NHS hospitals (which were located near the poorer areas), ability to pay and geographic access to services were not considered important explanatory factors. In the other study (Garlick et al, 1993), the analysis showed that a pregnant teenager living in London's Tower Hamlets was four times more likely to give birth than a pregnant teenager from Hampstead.

There are many examples of these simple mapping analyses in the research literature from other developed-world nations. In an Australian study (Evans, 2003) a clear urban/rural divide in teenage pregnancy was demonstrated, with inner Sydney having low rates, and higher rates found in remote areas. In some Australian outback towns, teenagers were 32 times more likely to become pregnant than their city-dwelling peers (PM, Australian Broadcasting Corporation, 2003). In Queensland, teenage fertility rates in the poorest areas have been found to be 10–20 times higher than rates in affluent areas (Coory, 2000). Area variation in teenage reproductive behaviour can also be seen in Canada and New Zealand (see Cheesbrough et al, 2002 for an overview).

The second group of studies includes those that might be considered more advanced in that authors have attempted to uncover the existence of area, neighbourhood or peer effects on outcomes, sometimes using qualitative as well as statistical methodologies (Crane, 1991; Evans et al, 1992; Sloggett and Joshi, 1998; Tabberer et al, 2000; McCulloch, 2001; Lee et al, 2004; Bradshaw et al, 2005; Arai, 2007; Maxwell and Chase, 2008). These studies are often informed by 'neighbourhood effects' and related theoretical approaches which derive from ecologically oriented theoretical perspectives on human behaviour (Bronfenbrenner, 1979). From this perspective, factors affecting teenage sexual and reproductive behaviour exist within the wider community or neighbourhood, within peer groups and within the family (Brindis, 2006). At the heart of this approach is the idea that neighbourhoods or communities can have impacts on behaviour that are independent of individual characteristics (such as SES) and that are generated primarily through an individual's social interaction with others in salient social contexts (Atkinson and Kintrea, 2001). Particularly within poor communities the effects of social interaction with others are likely to be stronger, given the lack of opportunities in such places and the paucity of positive role models of behaviour (Brewster, 1994; Sucoff and Upchurch, 1998; Burton and Jarrett, 2000; Dietz, 2002).

Within this body of work, some authors have highlighted the role that differential access to services plays in teenage pregnancy. In Bradshaw and colleagues' (2005) work on neighbourhood variation in teenage pregnancy and abortion, for example, deprivation (low income, unemployment, poor health) explained about three-quarters of the variance in teenage conception rates for 1997, and about three-quarters of the variance in abortion rates. There were a number of 'outliers' observed in the analysis – places that had either too-high or too-low rates based on socioeconomic profile, and where unexplained variation might be linked to local services. An analysis of variation in rates across the (former) Wessex Regional Health Authority showed that teenagers who lived 3–7 km from a youth-oriented clinic were 1.11 times more likely to conceive than those who lived 0–3 km away (Diamond et al, 1999). However, in an older analysis, a significant *positive* correlation (r=0.51) between teenage conceptions and the proportion of teenagers attending clinics was demonstrated (Wilson et al, 1992), and in a US study (Goodman et al, 2007) no significant relationship was found between geographic proximity to clinics and teenage pregnancy.

Local services are, of course, important in influencing reproductive outcomes, but the idea that some communities are *culturally* oriented to early child bearing is a powerful one hinted at in the TPS, and the possible existence of social or cultural factors influencing the timing of pregnancy is often suggested in spatial analyses of behaviour. Early motherhood may be more normative in some neighbourhoods than in others (Bauder, 2002), and this can be reinforced by the visibility of pregnant young women, or parenting teenagers, in the community (Anderson, 1991). Neighbourhood peers and school friends may also communicate positive messages about early pregnancy and parenthood (in the same way that they may exert pressure on friends to initiate sex) (Arai, 2007). In one analysis of qualitative data collected on a North Yorkshire council estate, anti-abortion sentiment deterred pregnant young women from seeking termination and effectively created a 'pro-early child bearing' local culture (Tabberer et al, 2000).

There is only a small body of work using qualitative methodologies on the transmission of fertility-related norms and values within peer and wider community networks in a British setting, but, considering the importance placed on peer influences on behaviour (Maxwell and Chase, 2008), more research remains to be done in this area.

Demographic

SES and geographic location are sometimes confounded with ethnicity (areas with high teenage pregnancy rates tend to be poorer, and some also have high proportions of minority ethnic populations. Southwark, in London, for example, has high rates of deprivation, an ethnically mixed population and high teenage fertility rates; Petersen et al, 2008). Yet, despite ethnicity appearing to be a significant variable, there is a lack of research on the experience of teenage pregnancy and fertility among British minority ethnic groups (Higginbottom et al, 2006), which may be attributable to deficiencies in the data available for analysis. The situation in the US is different. There, research on teenage pregnancy is often concerned with issues of ethnicity (Bonell, 2004), and there is a large body of work on the experience of African-American teenagers in particular (see, for example, Danziger, 1995) and, more recently, Hispanic teenagers (see, for example, Ryan et al, 2005).

Recognising the lack of research on ethnicity and teenage pregnancy, the TPU commissioned work on the experience of teenage pregnancy among British minority ethnic groups. One of these projects explored the experience of early parenthood in these populations. In many respects, the findings from this work are similar to those observed in research focused on the majority, white population. In particular, the authors flagged up the relatively positive ideas their respondents communicated about young parenthood:

> The findings of this study seem to indicate that the young people did not attach a fatalistic or inexorably negative view to the notion of becoming a parent early, and in some instances viewed the prospect of early parenthood more positively than current UK government strategy would suggest. (Higginbottom et al, 2008, p 97)

Respondents' diverse experiences of pregnancy and parenthood were significant; some parents were married, for example, and young age at child bearing was not seen as problematic from their community's perspective (Owen et al, 2008). The other TPU-commissioned project (Curtis et al, 2005; Sinha et al, 2006) focused on the sexual behaviour of young people of diverse minority ethnic status in East London.

The existence of community norms about the timing of child bearing was briefly discussed in an analysis of Labour Force Survey data (Berthoud, 2001), where differentials in teenage fertility by ethnic group were demonstrated with Black Caribbean, Bangladeshi and Pakistani women having higher rates than White or Indian women. Based on the situation of teenagers when they have their children (especially marriage patterns in their respective ethnic group), Caribbean, Pakistani and Bangladeshi teenagers were deemed to behave broadly within the 'expectations of their various cultural groups if they have children; whereas white teenagers are contradicting current normative expectations' (p 16).

There is a large body of research on the relationship between early conception and family-of-origin factors. Typically, it is family structure that is significantly correlated with teenage pregnancy, with girls from lone-parent backgrounds more likely to become pregnant than those from two-parent families. However, other dimensions of the family are also cited as important. In particular, the existence of intergenerational cycles of early child bearing (as evidenced by the age at which a teenager's mother began child bearing) has been explored in the literature, as have other aspects of family life, such as family functioning and parental supervision of teenagers.

The impact of family structure on teenage reproductive behaviour is a consistent theme in the research, and it is one that is closely aligned to SES (lone-parent families are usually poorer than two-parent families). Early sexual activity, pregnancy and parenthood are associated with growing up in a lone-parent family (Kiernan, 1997), although, apart from the link between this and deprivation, it is not clear what it is about family structure that affects sexual and reproductive behaviour. Early reproduction could be related to aspects of the parent–child relationship (Baumrind, 1971), such as the nature and scope of communication between parents and children (Wellings and Wadsworth, 1999) and reduced parental ability to monitor behaviour (East, 1999; Meade et al, 2008). In lone-parent families the relationship between the parent and child may be more strained than it is in two-parent families; there may be less time (because of work commitments) to foster positive family functioning, which affects the kind of communication between parent and child or a lone parent's ability to supervise their child's behaviour. Parents can 'shield' a teenager from too-early sexual behaviour. They can also play a pivotal role in promoting or hindering the transmission of wider values and norms about pregnancy and fertility (Furstenberg et al, 2000), maybe by example or by the degree of support offered to a pregnant or parenting teenager.

The age at which an individual's mother started child bearing is strongly correlated with teenage pregnancy. It is often observed that the daughter of a teenage mother is one and a half times more likely to become a young mother than the daughter of an older mother (SEU, 1999). In Bonell and colleagues' (2006) analysis of longitudinal data collected during evaluation of a sex education trial, teenagers from lone-parent families, or who had mothers who were teenagers when they were born, were more likely to report early sexual debut and conception by age 15/16. Kirkman et al (2001) observed that many of the women in their study of Australian teenage mothers came from family backgrounds where young motherhood was common. One respondent reported that: 'She (mum) had me when she was 19. Her mum had her when she was 17, and her mum had her when she was 19' (p 285). These authors do not discuss whether a tendency for young motherhood within the family of origin encourages teenagers to carry on a family tradition of early fertility or not. Rather, they suggest, the 'family canon' (a history of early fertility) provides the young women with an 'alternative plot' with which to counter dominant narratives about the inadvisability of teenage motherhood.

The existence of intergenerational cycles of early motherhood has been observed in populations elsewhere in the developed world. In one US study of Latina and African-American families (East et al, 2007), compared with young women with no family history of teenage births, young women whose sister had had a teenage birth and those whose sister *and* mother had both given birth as teenagers were significantly more likely to experience a teenage pregnancy (OR 4.8 and 5.1, respectively). The association persisted even after controlling for SES and mothers' parenting characteristics. In another US study (Meade et al, 2008), an ecological approach was used to explore intergenerational cycles of teenage fertility in a sample of nearly 1,500 individuals in the National Longitudinal Survey of Youth. The daughters of teenage mothers were 66% more likely to become teenage mothers, after controlling for other risks.

There is a growing body of literature on the effects of pathological family functioning, including sexual and physical abuse and neglect, on teenagers' sexual and reproductive behaviour (Blinn-Pike et al, 2002;

Erdmans and Black, 2008; Senn et al, 2008). In a British analysis of the link between child sexual abuse (occurring before 13 years) and factors such as later mental health and parenting behaviours (Roberts et al, 2004), sexual abuse was associated with negative outcomes in adulthood as well as teenage pregnancy, even after adjustment for other adverse childhood experiences.

Research from other countries has confirmed the relationship between teenage pregnancy and abuse in childhood. In Romans and colleagues' (1997) New Zealand-based study, four factors predicted teenage pregnancy: living in a non-intact family; having parents who argued; being physically punished after age 12; and not having had a confidante during childhood. Serious sexual assault (rape) predicted early pregnancy independently of these four variables. In (what is possibly) the first study from a Latin American country to demonstrate a relationship between childhood abuse and adolescent pregnancy, Pallitto and Murillo (2008) analysed data from nearly 4,000 El Salvadoran women aged between 15 and 24 and found that women who were sexually or physically abused, or who experienced any type of abuse, had a 48%, 42% and 31% higher risk respectively of early pregnancy than women not reporting abuse. This relationship remained after adjustment for confounding factors.

Although the ways in which young women respond to sexual abuse vary (clearly, not all will experience a teenage pregnancy), there does appear to be a 'pathway' from sexual abuse to reproductive outcomes that can be clearly seen in the lives of abused young women who experience early pregnancy. This was succinctly described by US researchers (Erdmans and Black, 2008) as a pathway that

> tends to follow a well-trod trajectory: sexual assault as a child, precocious and risky sexual behavior as an adolescent, withdrawal from school, abuse of alcohol and drugs, and finally pregnancy and adolescent motherhood. (p 78)

Psycho-social

The psychologically oriented research links teenage sexual behaviour, pregnancy and parenthood to factors such as a lack of self-esteem, emotional problems and having an external locus of control (Vernon et al, 1983; Drummond and Hansford, 1990; Kiernan, 1997). In some of this work, sexual activity and pregnancy is also linked to high-risk behaviours such as alcohol (Coleman and Cater, 2005) and drug use and aggressive behaviour (Valois et al, 1999).

While the research on the psycho-social correlates of early conception and fertility is relatively peripheral within mainstream accounts of teenage pregnancy (Coley and Chase-Lansdale, 1998), the belief in a link between teenage pregnancy and self-esteem, in particular, has become more widely accepted. The idea that early sexual activity and pregnancy is linked to low self-esteem became fashionable in the latter half of the 20th century, particularly in the US (Baumeister et al, 2005). Young women with low self-esteem are believed to have sex when they do not want it, making them more vulnerable to pregnancy and leading to high levels of regret (Doskoch, 2007). Yet, in a systematic review of the relationship between self-esteem and teenagers' sexual behaviours, attitudes and intentions (which analysed findings from 38 publications) 62% of behavioural findings and 72% of the attitudinal findings exhibited no statistically significant association (Goodson et al, 2006). Baumeister and colleagues' (2005) debunking of some of the myths around self-esteem led them to conclude that:

> All in all, the results do not support the idea that low self-esteem predisposes young people to more or earlier sexual activity. If anything, those with high self-esteem are less inhibited, more willing to disregard risks and more prone to engage in sex. At the same time, bad sexual experiences and unwanted pregnancies appear to lower self-esteem. (p 55)

Self-esteem may have only marginal importance to sexual behaviour and reproductive outcomes, but there appears to be a correlation between the often fatalistic 'mindset' of working-class and disadvantaged youth and teenage pregnancy. Policy makers often describe the relationship between the 'low expectations' apparently evinced by youth from less-advantaged backgrounds and early fertility (SEU, 1999), but rarely demonstrate a real understanding of what this means. Qualitative researchers, in contrast, have evocatively described working-class young people's experience of low expectations, how this is manifested in their values and behaviour and how it is at odds with prevailing middle-class beliefs. In a study of young people living in diverse English communities, Thomson (2000), speaking of a middle-class community's values, notes that:

> The kind of individualized cultural and social capital which accrued to young people at Forest Green [school in a wealthy area] is not just portable, but is necessarily portable. It demands social and geographic mobility to

be realised. Not only is it worthless in the here and now, but it is threatened by the competing forms of value that dominate the here and now – sexiness, fitness, risk taking and 'experience'. While young people are already middle class, to remain so requires that they invest in the future rather than the present and that they avoid the public spaces of the local. (p 418)

The present-oriented and localised 'sexiness, fitness, risk taking and experience' values referred to by Thomson is a reminder that young women (and men) from disadvantaged backgrounds *do* appear to have a different perspective on life, a 'limited' sense of life's possibilities or 'limited' temporal horizons. This, of course, may be an entirely accurate reading of their prospects (Geronimus, 1997). Importantly here, limited temporal horizons (or 'discounting the future') affect perceptions about the optimal time for child bearing. Chesson and colleagues (2006) showed that young women who engaged in riskier sexual behaviours and pregnancy as teenagers were likely to have high rates of temporal discounting. The family-building intentions of working-class youth often appear accelerated, compared with those of their middle-class counterparts (Geronimus, 1997). In Jewell and colleagues' (2000) study, working-class women considered the age range 17–25 to be the optimal age for child bearing. Their middle-class counterparts reported late 20s or early 30s as the best age. In an analysis of NCDS data (Kiernan, 1997), women who became teenage mothers were more likely to express pro-early parenthood and marriage views at age 16 than those women who did not become teenage mothers. Among women who became teenage mothers, 9% reported wanting to start a family before age 19 and 30% expressed a desire to marry before age 19, compared with 2% and 14% of older mothers respectively.

Disadvantaged young women, or those from working-class backgrounds, may express an earlier ideal age to start child bearing, and they also appear to have an altogether more laissez faire view of pregnancy (Morehead and Soriano, 2005). The idea that pregnancy and child bearing falls neatly into 'planned/unplanned', 'wanted/unwanted' categories limits our understanding of teenagers' reproductive intentions and behaviours. In a Canadian exploration (Kives and Jamieson, 2001) of pregnancy intentions among teenage mothers-to-be, 22 women had 'sort of' or 'really wanted' to be pregnant, 32 did not want to be pregnant and four said they did not care. Forty-two said they were happy to be pregnant.

Young fathers and looked-after children and young people

This chapter, like most of the book, is focused on women, mothers and motherhood, primarily because this is where the policy and research focus has traditionally lain (Gelder, 2002; Glikman, 2004; Whitehead, 2008). There are two groups discussed here that have not figured (until relatively recently, at least) prominently in the research literature, but that are important to an understanding of teenage pregnancy: young fathers; and children and young people who have experienced the care system. From a research perspective, young fathers have traditionally been ignored, perceived as irrelevant, as lacking commitment or as not available to be researched (Gelder, 2002). This is a serious omission, given their importance to the well-being of their partners and children. Similarly, young people who have been in the care system are likely to experience many of the risk factors associated with teenage pregnancy (low SES, poor educational attainment) yet, until fairly recently, there was little research on their experience of pregnancy and parenthood.

There has been a growth in the academic literature on young fathers which focuses on their socio-demographic characteristics, their experience of fatherhood and issues around service access and needs. This development reflects a more general increase in interest in fatherhood, as well as concern about teenage parenthood. In *Teenage Pregnancy*, young men were identified as 'half of the problem and solution' to teenage pregnancy (Gelder, 2002).

Men who father children with teenage mothers are not necessarily teenagers themselves. In the US and the UK, men who father children with teenage mothers typically tend to be a few years older than their partners, and a minority may be significantly older (Bunting and McAuley, 2004; Whitehead, 2008). The age gap between teenage mothers and much older partners has prompted moves in the US to prosecute older men who father children with teenagers under statutory rape laws (Lindberg et al, 1997). Growing awareness of the age gap between teenage mothers and their partners has helped to raise knowledge of sexual health and other risks associated with teenage girls having older sexual partners (Manlove et al, 2006).

In many respects, the socio-demographic profile of young and teenage fathers is similar to that of teenage mothers. Young fathers tend to be from low SES backgrounds and have lower educational attainment and fewer employment opportunities than their non-parenting peers (Reeves, 2006). They may also have similar mental health profiles to teenage mothers (Quinlivan and Condon, 2005), and have experienced adversity as children (Anda et al, 2001). Tan and Quinlivan (2006) found that fathers who sired children with teenage mothers were more likely to report adverse early family relationships, such as exposure to domestic violence or parental separation or divorce.

Reeves (2006, 2007) documented the transition to fatherhood among vulnerable and excluded young men. For some of her respondents, the birth of their child made the young men face up to responsibilities and alter their reckless behaviour:

> It [the birth of my children] just made me realise there is ... more responsibilities, I was going to be a father. I needed to try and make sure that my partner and children was safe and secure. And that if they ever needed me, they could always come to me. I think that made me realise that it was time to sort my life out and get me act together.... things like going out and driving around in my car like a maniac, I stopped. ('Manuel' in Reeves, 2006, p 87)

Seen this way, imminent fatherhood appears to have a similar effect to the one that motherhood can have on young women (McDermott et al, 2004; Rolfe, 2008). Young fathers' relationship with their children can be related to the strength of their attachment to the mother of their children. In US research of 109 poor, young fathers' involvement with their children (Gavin et al, 2002), paternal involvement was predicted most strongly by the quality of the parents' romantic relationship. The father's employment status, the maternal grandmother's education and the father's relationship with the baby's maternal grandmother were also associated with paternal involvement.

Attempts to better integrate young fathers into service development and provision are to be welcomed. Sure Start Plus (SSP) is aimed at young fathers as well as mothers, although its evaluation showed that many service providers did not think that young fathers were well catered for within it (Wiggins et al, 2005). The evaluators found that, in the first two years of SSP, few programmes worked with young fathers, although, over the lifetime of SSP, more started working with young fathers either individually, with their partners or in groups. By the third year, all programme coordinators reported that they thought it important to work with young fathers and two-thirds of the programmes had strategies in place to undertake work with them. However, as the evaluators note, work with young fathers remains a secondary priority within most programmes, and more needs to be done to ascertain young fathers' needs and barriers to service use.

The second traditionally overlooked group in the literature on teenage pregnancy is young women and men who have experienced being looked after in the care system. Many of the factors associated with teenage pregnancy and parenthood described above coalesce in young people who have been looked after. Young people who have experienced the care system tend to come from lower SES backgrounds, to have lived in lone-parent families, to have lower rates of educational attainment and to have experienced childhood adversity (which may have led to their being placed in the care system). Given this, it is hardly surprising that a high proportion of young women and men who are, or have been, in the care system experience early pregnancy and parenthood (SCIE, 2004/5). In one study (Garnett, 1992) of 135 children leaving care in three English local authorities, one in seven of the girls were either pregnant or had already become mothers at the time of discharge from care.

Among looked-after young people, it is not clear which factors significantly influence reproductive outcomes. Is it the ones mentioned above – low SES and lack of educational attainment – for example, or is it something about being in the care system itself (Barn and Mantovani, 2007)? There may not be a large body of research on teenage pregnancy among individuals who have been in care, but, in the research that has been done, there is a tendency to see the experience of early pregnancy and parenthood in this group as a consequence of lack of access to information and inadequate sexual health knowledge. Being in the care system may mean that young people are not exposed to adequate sexual health education and advice, and this may make them more vulnerable to early pregnancy (Chase et al, 2006). This is probably true, but it is often the experience of adversity, in either early or later childhood, that is the most significant factor in relation to sexual and reproductive behaviour.

Alongside recognition of the role that access to information and services plays in early pregnancy, there is sometimes in the literature an acknowledgement that teenage pregnancy is linked to the idea of 'compensation' for adversity experienced in childhood, that young people want to 'make up' for something that they lacked as children (Barn and Mantovani, 2007). Research on young people who have been in the care system highlights the many ways in which they attempt to 'make good' in the face of barriers and the trauma of early-life adversity. Making good often entails trying to secure the love they did not get from their own parents, either through sexual activity or through child bearing. Maxwell and Chase (2008) maintain that young people who have been in care report different kinds of pressure:

pressure to find love to replace that lost from their own parenting experiences; pressure to be sexually active due to a lack of boundaries set in the residential care homes in which they lived; pressure in relation to the decision as to whether or not to continue with or terminate the pregnancy; and pressure due to the stigma associated with being a care leaver on what life aspirations were acceptable and realistic. A further pressure … [is] to be 'better' parents than their peers and their own parents. (p 307)

For young people who have experienced the care system and have suffered the worst kinds of early-life adversity, early child bearing can represent, in some respects, a chance to *rewrite* their own histories (SmithBattle, 2000). Pregnancy and child bearing against a backdrop of early life adversity can represent a positive choice, an opportunity for young people to construct a meaningful identity and alternative 'vocation' in the face of limited opportunities. From this perspective, it might be seen as a rational behaviour (Arai, 2003; McDermott et al, 2004) and as a sign of rapid maturity. In Erdmans and Black's (2008) study of teenage mothers who had experienced sexual abuse, the experiences of one young mother who had been raped and become a drug user were such that, by the age of just 17, 'she felt as if she had lived 39 years. "I've been through so much. I've done some things that older people haven't even done yet.... I been through a lot"' (p 84).

Summary

There is a large body of research on the factors associated with teenage pregnancy and fertility. In the research literature examined here factors associated with both outcomes fell broadly into structural, demographic and psycho-social categories. This overview confirms findings from other reviews (for example, Imamura et al, 2007), principally in that teenage pregnancy and child bearing can be seen to be concentrated among low SES groups (whether measured by social class status, housing or geographic location) and among young women who have experienced low educational attainment or disengagement from the education system. Teenage mothers are also more likely to come from lone-parent families, and/or families that have a tradition of early fertility (among mothers and siblings). In addition, young people who have experienced adversity in early life (especially being in the care system) have a higher risk of early pregnancy. And, while teenage pregnancy may be non-normative among majority white populations in the developed world, some minority ethnic groups in the same countries appear to have above-average rates of teenage fertility. In these communities, though, early child bearing within marriage is sometimes encouraged and does not have the negative connotations attached to it that it might have in the majority population.

The overview of the research here reveals clusters of factors, observable at macro and micro level, associated with teenage pregnancy and fertility. Yet, at the same time, and while recognising that there are commonalities of experience (across different countries, in different population samples), it helps not to paint with too broad a brushstroke. There will be differences among the kinds of young women who become pregnant or who become teenage mothers.

Although the international research has not been explored systematically here, it is clear that many of the same factors associated with teenage pregnancy in, for example, the US are the same as in the UK. Yet research on the *consequences* of early motherhood (Berthoud and Iacovou, 2002) shows that these appear highly dependent on national context, suggesting that teenage motherhood is more normative and less stigmatised in some places, or that welfare states respond to it in different ways (maybe by provision of education to teenage mothers, or by access to enhanced welfare benefits) (Nativel and Daguerre, 2006). It may also suggest that the risk factors associated with teenage pregnancy and motherhood vary geographically, possibly in subtle ways, but in ways that make its consequences more or less damaging according to the setting in which these outcomes occur.

Notes
[1] Vicki Pollard is a teenage mother character in the popular BBC comedy show *Little Britain*.

[2] Children and young people who are 'looked after in the care system' are those who do not normally reside with one or both biological parents and are either in the care of the local authority or in foster care.

THREE

Epidemics, fluctuations and trends: the everyday depiction of teenage pregnancy

Introduction

Contemporary forms of media are diverse. Internet-based news and information sites, weblogs and podcasts, as well as traditional television programmes, newspapers and magazines, cater for fragmented and varied audiences and have the potential to reach large numbers of people. In this kind of environment, it might be expected that multifaceted and alternative stories of teenage pregnancy and motherhood would emerge. Yet the expansion of media outlets has led not to a greater diversification of stories about teenage pregnancy, but to a *multiplication* of negative stories about it and how the 'problem' urgently needs to be addressed. In one analysis of BBC Online content, nearly 60% of 162 news items had a focus on the prevention of teenage pregnancy (Shaw and Lawlor, 2007).

While the focus of stories on teenage pregnancy is largely on its negative aspects, the tone of reporting is invariably sensational, sometimes even salacious (Selman, 1998/2001; Simey and Wellings, 2008) – although many issues are dealt with similarly in the British media, and teenage pregnancy is not unique in this respect. The job of newspaper proprietors is to sell newspapers, and teenage sexuality, in its many forms, helps to do this. However, given that most people's perceptions of pregnant and parenting teenagers derive *entirely* from media sources (and rarely from experience), one consequence of contemporary modes of reporting on teenage pregnancy is a distorted public understanding of its scale. The gap between the actual size of the teenage parent population and commonly held beliefs about its size must be one of the greatest observed. In one study of public attitudes to lone parents, over one-fifth of respondents believed that 40% of lone parents are teenagers. The real figure is 3% (RBS, 2003).

This 'myth–reality' gap arises in part because journalists covering teenage pregnancy and, through them, their readers, often fail to understand the implications of the figures they are presented with and will readily accept their validity without proper consideration. An inability on the part of people who are not statisticians to gauge the size of the pregnant or parenting adolescent population is understandable. However, a failure to appreciate the scale of teenage pregnancy is not the only effect of salacious media coverage on our understanding of teenage pregnancy. Contemporary reporting of teenage pregnancy also has another baleful consequence: it generates and reinforces negative attitudes towards pregnant and parenting teenagers, and compounds young mothers' own sense of having 'transgressed' wider social norms governing the timing of child bearing. The production of teenage pregnancy as a problem in the media, and its consumption by the public, cannot be easily dismissed as an example of harmless provision of news or information; it has implications for the well-being of young women and their families. It is not unreasonable to suggest that media-generated images of youthful pregnancy are pivotal in the creation of negative public attitudes to teenage mothers.

In this chapter, the myth–reality gap on teenage pregnancy is explored by focusing on contemporary British media representations of youthful pregnancy. There is a brief exploration of the ways in which data on teenage pregnancy are used in everyday media and then, in greater detail, a discussion of the kind of stories told about pregnant and parenting teenagers by journalists. Focusing largely on mainstream (print and online) media coverage in the first decade of the 21st century, the analysis here is not exhaustive or systematic, and it is not meant to be. It is a starting point only, and much work remains to be done on understanding popular representations of pregnant and parenting teenagers, how these have changed over time as the media has expanded and diversified, and the effects of this on young mothers.

The uses of data

The depiction of teenage pregnancy in the media (and, to a greater degree, this is also true of the treatment of teenage pregnancy in the academic and policy literature) is driven by the collection, analysis and production of demographic and other data or research findings. It is the release of new analyses of data, usually conception rates, that causes a flurry of newspaper articles about teenage pregnancy. These data are held to be inarguable proof that youthful pregnancy is a problem. Given this, it might be argued that the public (through the press) receive an accurate and fair picture of teenage pregnancy, a picture reflecting high academic standards, or one that is even 'evidence-based' (Graham and McDermott, 2005).Yet, data are not always reliable, and academic research is not always objective and impartial, appropriately critical, rigorously executed and methodologically robust. Academics do not always scrutinise the taken–for–granted categories they are working with.The relationship between the academy, government and lobbying groups with an interest in policy making further complicates things. Research often reflects policy makers' concerns, and policy makers have tended, since the 1970s, to see youthful pregnancy as a pressing social problem. The journalistic 'product' we see in newspapers and online will have passed through many stages and processes before it appears in print or on the screen.The end product is a highly filtered one; this is particularly the case where newly available data or other research is used to build a story about teenage pregnancy.

Putting aside issues of how data or other research came to be generated in the first place, and what processes have been involved in getting it to the dissemination stage, the ways that data – and this is more relevant to analyses of demographic data rather than other research findings – on teenage pregnancy are used in everyday media stories make the 'problem' look worse than it is in reality.There are at least four ways in which this is commonly done.

First, data are often decontextualised by being presented without reference to a population at risk.These simple counts are therefore not 'anchored' and, where they are higher than previously, the impression is created that the events in question are increasing. For example, the *Telegraph* reported a 'sharp rise in under 16 pregnancy rates' in early 2007. The latest conception figures (2005) had just been published, showing an increase in the numbers of girls aged under 16 becoming pregnant. The paper made much of the fact that around 300 more girls in 2005 than in 2004 became pregnant in that age group. In fact, this equated to a very small change in the rate, from 7.5 to 7.8 per conceptions per 1,000. Similarly, in *Teenage Pregnancy*, the authors reported an analysis of 1997 data showing that there were an estimated 87,000 children with teenage mothers in England and Wales.This figure was widely reported in the press and elsewhere, and was still quoted a decade later.Yet, in a later study using 2001 data (Shaw and Lawlor, 2007) it was estimated that there were around 30,000 teenage mothers in the population, and births to teenage mothers constituted just 2% of all births.This makes the 87,000 figure look excessively large. Even if it were accurate, births to teenagers would still have comprised a small proportion of all births in that year.

There is nothing inherently wrong with counts; they are a useful measure of the scale of a behaviour or outcome in a specific population and are used to provide an indication of the resources needed to address it. Rates are more often used in relation to the implementation of the first aim of the Teenage Pregnancy Strategy (TPS), the prevention of teenage pregnancy, rather than the second, the provision of employment and educational opportunities for young mothers. To ensure the latter, reliable counts of the population are needed rather than rates (Shaw and Lawlor, 2007).

Second, changes to small numbers can look big when expressed as a percentage. Only a small number of girls under the age of 14 become pregnant every year in England and Wales, and most opt for termination of pregnancy. In June 2008, newly released abortion data showed that abortions to under-14s had increased (the *Mail Online* reported that for under-14 girls these had '*soared* by 21 per cent'[1]). In fact, this 21% was made up of the difference between the 2006 figure of 135 abortions and the 2007 figure of 163 – just 28 abortions.

Third, short-term changes are examined. Definitions of 'short-term' vary, but quarterly or six-monthly figures are often seized upon as evidence that a strategy is working (or not). This is not helpful where numbers are small to begin with, possibly because events at a low level of geography are being examined (for example, conceptions to under-16s at ward level). Even annual changes to rates do not give a fair picture of overall trends (again, particularly where numbers are low to begin with or the geographical level of analysis is small). Changes in trends from one year to the next are not always useful and could be ascribed to random statistical variation.

Fourth, comparisons with other countries are made to reinforce the perception that the UK is 'behind' other nations in relation to teenage pregnancy. The problems with the use of comparative data in the TPS and elsewhere will be described further in Chapter Six. In brief, these comparisons are often inappropriate because they do not compare like with like. The UK's teenage pregnancy rate, for example, is often compared with that of the Netherlands, a much smaller country with a large Catholic population and one with a low level of income inequality (the latter is strongly correlated with teenage fertility). In addition, no information is presented on how data on teenage pregnancy and fertility are collected in other countries. International differences in what kinds of data are collected, and how they are collected, can be substantial enough that quite elaborate statistical adjustments have to be performed before cross-national comparisons can be made (see Unicef, 2001, for example).

Media representations of teenage pregnancy rely only partly on the use of numbers. Depictions of teenage pregnancy as problematic are most vivid, and memorable, when words and phrases – sometimes alongside statistical information, and maybe even photographic images – are used to tell the story.

Stories about teenage pregnancy

It is recognised here that it is quite common to see 'discourses' in everything, especially in representations of, or policy responses to, teenage pregnancy (Kelly, 1996; Carabine, 2007; Duncan, 2007) as well as other social 'problems'. This observation is not meant to detract from work which attempts to 'unpack' the meanings attached to teenage pregnancy. However, as Duncan (2007) has observed, we need to build on these beginnings and start to develop a more advanced conceptual framework to properly understand depictions of, and policy responses to, teenage pregnancy. He sees three discourses in policies around teenage parenting: discourse as moral panic; discourse as quantitative social science; and the social exclusion discourse in New Labour policy. He further observes that:

> while each explanation may be a starting point, left standing alone discourse explanations can become simply shorthand for 'ways of talking' … The links between these conversations and how particular policy around teenage parenting is formulated remain to be established. Nor should we see policy makers as simply implementing 'discourse' in some unmediated way … (p 321)

Beating the odds

Here, the representation of teenage pregnancy in the British media in the early years of the new millennium is considered to be dominated by two principal discourses, one more common than the other. The first widely occurring and entrenched discourse is 'Teenage pregnancy as calamity'. This can be seen in media coverage of teenage pregnancy and is present in academic and policy outputs, although the language is less controversial. This is discussed in detail below. The second discourse, where teenage mothers are described as 'Beating the odds', is rarer but can still be seen in the media and, in modified form, can be a feature of the more 'revisionist' academic work on teenage pregnancy (Arai, 2003; McDermott et al, 2004). Sometimes elements of both can be seen in the same story.

Both discourses focus on the negative aspects of teenage pregnancy and motherhood – its association with poverty, with lack of education and opportunities, and poor or even abusive family backgrounds – but in the 'Beating the odds' discourse the story is tilted so that teenage pregnancy appears as an event that can 'rescue' a young woman from a difficult past and provide the catalyst for positive change. In this way, young mothers have overcome the odds against them and not turned out 'bad', as expected, but have become instead 'good' mothers, and sometimes even good students or good workers as well.

The 'Beating the odds' discourse can typically be seen in reports or articles in which the author begins by asking readers to suspend judgements about teenage mothers. He or she may then claim to have found proof that 'their' teenage mothers are different from those elsewhere (imagined or real). Their mothers are not whey-faced and overweight, but are often 'beautiful' and even 'delicate'. (On 22 July 2007, the *Sunday Times* carried a photograph on its magazine cover of a pregnant 15-year-old, who was described by the author of the article as 'strikingly beautiful' and as possessing 'delicacy'.) These mothers have made a success of their lives, despite early disadvantages. In the same *Sunday Times* article, entitled 'The truth about gymslip mothers' with the subtitle 'A climate of moral panic surrounds the issue of teenage motherhood. But should we be in such a rush to condemn it?', the author, on the subject of one of her interviewees, 'Coral', writes:

> For a girl like Coral, motherhood is a solution where there are no others; it's not her child that holds her back, it is her grisly history … A few months ago I would have automatically assumed a beleaguered girl like this to be an unfit mother, her child better off elsewhere. The informed picture is more complex, and now I am far less sure. 'Kacie has given me something to live for,' she says. 'Before I had nothing … I had no plans, no discipline, no-one to tell me what to do, or guide me.' How can it be that I am pleased that Coral has her daughter, a blameless child born into cramped, penurious, uncertain beginnings, but also into love? Because with Kacie … her mother nurtures at least a hope of making a life, and even a second-chance childhood, for both of them.

In this story, we see that Coral's child (Kacie) has 'saved her' from her blighted past. Before her birth, there was 'nothing', not even vague plans. Coral and Kacie's material and social circumstances are 'uncertain', but all that matters is Coral's love for her daughter. Coral's daughter is her 'second chance'. Similarly, in an earlier story covered in a special BBC Online report created in response to the publication of *Teenage Pregnancy*, the author introduces us to 'Maya', described as 'no "typical" teenage mum':

> Despite – or perhaps because of – the challenges, Maya has thrived. She has stretched her £85 a week to make a cheerful, comfortable home of her council flat in north London. The living room is filled with Jake's [son's] toys – a small plastic car, piles of blocks … She also ended her relationship with Terry [partner] about eight months ago. He had been in and out of prison since she was pregnant … Maya maintains that her story is a textbook case of triumph over adversity. She says she has strength because she's had no other choice. 'I'm strong because of all I've been through,' she said. 'I have got things to do and there is no going back.'[2]

While any attempt to interrogate stereotypes is to be welcomed, this kind of approach to teenage mothers is undermined not only by its sentimentality but also by the assumption, implicit in these accounts, that only teenage mothers are 'saved' from difficult pasts by parenthood. As Macintyre and Cunningham-Burley (1993) have observed, all kinds of motivations for becoming a parent are ascribed to women aged under 20, and held to be unique to them alone when they may also be present in women aged over 20 as well. To admit this would undermine the depiction of teenage mothers as a distinct population and reduce the newspaper story to the commonplace. The presentation of teenage mothers as different and distinct from the rest of the population is reinforced by the authors describing teenage mothers as one might another form of life, as classical anthropologists did of the natives they were geographically and socially distant from. In this way, the journalist makes a distinction between herself and her interviewees, between her interviewees and her readers.

Teenage pregnancy as calamity

Relentless rise in teenage pregnancies

The number of teenage pregnancies has risen again despite an expensive Government campaign to lower them. There were 42,200 pregnancies among under-18s in England and Wales in 2003 … up by 200 on the previous year. (*Daily Mail*, 25 February 2005)

Battle to cut teenage pregnancy rate

Britain has become notorious for having the highest teenage pregnancy rate in western Europe, twice that of Germany, three times higher than France and six times that of the Netherlands. While the rest of the continent has seen dramatic falls in teenage parenthood since the early 80s, the UK has long been the exception … (*Guardian*, 22 February 2001)

Pregnant at 11 and 'happy to be a mum'

A 12-year-old girl will become Britain's youngest mother when she gives birth next month. She became pregnant at the age of 11 when she lost her virginity to a 15-year-old boy during a drunken night out. Police said yesterday that the boy had been charged with rape … The girl … smokes 20 cigarettes a day but has insisted she is ready for motherhood. 'I didn't think I'd get pregnant because it was my first time, but I'm really excited and looking forward to being a mum,' she said. '… I think I'll be able to cope as I've had lots of practice looking after my brothers …' The girl's mother, who is supporting her daughter, is 34 and has an eight-month-old baby boy of her own. She said: 'I'm not ashamed of my daughter. In fact, I'm proud of her for keeping her baby.' The girl left school after being excluded for fighting. (*Daily Telegraph*, 15 May 2006)[3]

Britain second worst country for schoolgirl pregnancies

Britain has the second highest teenage birth rate in the developed world, exceeded only by America, a United Nations report said yesterday … The survey of 28 developed countries found that, while teenage pregnancies had fallen by up to 75 per cent in many industrialised nations, Britain still had an 'alarmingly high' rate … (*Daily Telegraph*, 30 May 2002)

The puzzle of teenagers and sex

Despite every effort over many years, the level of teenagers having sex and getting pregnant is as high as ever. And nobody really knows why ... (BBC News Online, Friday, 12 March 2004)

Children of nine may get sex advice packs

[A British MP says] large parts of the country are 'blighted' by high teenage pregnancy levels which create a 'vicious cycle of under-achievement, benefit dependency, ill health, lack of aspiration, poor parenting and child poverty'. (*Daily Telegraph*, 28 January 2008)

The snippets here – taken from newspapers in print and online in the first decade of the 21st century – are broadly typical of the coverage of teenage sexuality, pregnancy and parenthood in the British press and illustrate the diverse ways these aspects of teenage behaviour are portrayed as a problem. They are also used here to demonstrate how teenage pregnancy is 'calamity', the first, and more significant, discourse. If the idea of teenage pregnancy as calamity sounds too strong, consider research undertaken by Whitehead (2001) on the stigma attached to early pregnancy. Her analysis of qualitative data from pregnant and non-pregnant British teenagers demonstrated a belief among respondents that early pregnancy and motherhood could lead to 'social death'. The young Canadian mothers in a study of stigma (Whitley and Kirmayer, 2008) were not even teenagers when they gave birth, yet they reported experiencing the worst forms of social stigma: 'Feelings of guilt, shame, humiliation, pain and internal conflict associated with "young" motherhood seemed to dominate younger Anglophone Euro-Canadian participants' lives ...' (p 345).

Based on the reports above, teenage sexual and reproductive behaviour can be seen as problematic for myriad reasons. For one, the apparently inexorable increase in youthful pregnancy rates cannot be properly stemmed (rates are described as rising 'relentlessly'. In other reports, they can be 'soaring', or 'going through the roof', or simply 'rising', 'stalling' or 'plateauing'. Rates can also be 'at record levels', or simply 'worrying' or 'escalating,' and in need of being 'cut' or 'slashed'). Or, teenage pregnancy is problematic because the 'mysterious' nature of youthful sexuality confounds efforts to deal with it (battle imagery is frequently used in these reports– it is a 'battle' to deal with teenage pregnancy, or sometimes a 'war', and sexual health workers are often described as being at the 'front line'). Moreover, the most troublesome aspects of teenage sexuality 'blight' the lives of even the youngest, most vulnerable, adolescents. And a high prevalence of teenage pregnancy – for which Britain has attained notoriety among its European neighbours – is a cause of national shame (Britain is 'worst').

At a glance, we can also see in these media snippets the main features of what has been described as the 'epidemic' depiction of teenage pregnancy. The history of teenage pregnancy as an epidemic has been well documented (Richan, 1987; Luker, 1996; Hacking, 1999) and can be traced back to 1976, when the Alan Guttmacher Institute published the booklet *11 million teenagers: What can be done about the epidemic of adolescent pregnancies in the United States*. The 'discovery' of teenage pregnancy as a problem in the US in the 1970s owes much to this publication, which is still regularly cited as a landmark report on adolescent sexual and reproductive behaviour. From an epidemic perspective, teenage pregnancy is a kind of blight with a viral-like nature, one that is essentially unknowable, yet capable of spreading itself through a youthful population and able to withstand efforts to defeat it. Moreover, as a geographically bounded 'catastrophe', its existence marks a nation out as distinctive and different from its neighbours. Seen in this way, teenage pregnancy becomes a dangerous entity that seems to have arisen from nowhere.

As noted earlier, the use of emotive and sensational language by journalists to describe socially proscribed behaviour is not confined to teenage pregnancy: moral panics in the media and elsewhere have been the subjects of academic analysis ever since the idea was first articulated (Cohen, 1972). At different times and in different ways, Blacks, Travellers (especially of the New Age variety), benefit claimants and, most recently, Eastern European migrants (Pijpers, 2006), have been the subject of moral panics.

However, we can see in media coverage of teenage pregnancy something of its 'exceptionalism' when compared with these other groups. The methods used to describe marginalised groups in the media are broadly similar to those used for sexually active, pregnant or parenting teenagers. Stylistically, the same devices may be used – sensational and emotive language, including heavy use of metaphors, with images of chaos and blight evoked. Yet, in some respects, popular representations of pregnant and parenting teenagers are distinct from those of other socially ostracised groups. The language used and imagery evoked are such as to suggest that there can be few population subgroups who appear to embody so many social and moral 'evils'. It is as if pregnant and parenting teenagers represent all the bad things in society.

The 'epidemic' idea of teenage pregnancy is subsumed within the 'Teenage pregnancy as calamity' discourse, since the latter is less about contagion per se (though this is an element of it) and more about a generalised sense of chaos: conception is bad for the teenage girl herself, for her baby, her partner, her family, her community and, importantly, society (and even the future of society). In this way, calamity spreads out into personal, familial, geographical and temporal spheres. Calamity is a broad category encompassing all kinds of evils: welfare dependency; rampant sexuality; poor parenting; residence in poor neighbourhoods. Teenage pregnancy can be either the cause of these things, or their consequence. It is the association that is important, not the causal pathways.

Teenage pregnancy is represented as calamity in the ways described above: through use of emotive language, and also through the selective use or interpretation of data and (much less frequently) the use of photographic images. Other techniques may also be used in conjunction with these. One widely used one is to 'intensify' teenage pregnancy as a problem. A problem can be a problem on its own, but can be intensified as such if placed next to other problems. This is achieved by juxtaposing teenage pregnancy with unavowedly negative social or health phenomena. In the case of sexually transmitted infection (STI), for example, this can only ever be a problem. By placing teenage pregnancy with STI in a newspaper story, teenage pregnancy also comes to be seen also as a wholly negative phenomenon. In this kind of story, the endpoints are forgotten: STIs lead to scarring, pain, infertility, morbidity and even death, while pregnancy ends with a baby.

In the 'Teenage pregnancy as calamity' discourse, core, negative phrases are used repeatedly. This has the effect of reinforcing dominant views of teenage pregnancy and can lead to the generation of stock phrases, which acquire a conversational currency of their own in everyday social interactions. One that has passed down into many reports and journal papers, magazines and newspapers, and which can be heard on televised discussions of teenage pregnancy, is a statement used in *Teenage Pregnancy*: 'It seems as if sex is compulsory and contraception forbidden.' An oft-used one in the US, and to a lesser extent in the UK, is 'Kids having kids' or 'Babies having babies' (which is odd, considering that most teenage mothers are adults). Heilborn and colleagues (2007) link the beginning of the social construction of teenage pregnancy as a problem in Brazil to an influential article written by the Minister of Health, entitled 'Child-mothers'.

The spectre of the underclass

The exceptionalism of teenage pregnancy, at least in respect of its representation in the media, is often linked to the idea of an 'underclass' (Murray, 1990). Few newspaper or media reports refer specifically to the underclass when reporting on teenage pregnancy, yet, without necessarily referring to it, the underclass, with all its dark and dangerous attributes, is strongly brought to mind in these descriptions of teenage sexual and reproductive behaviour. The newspaper report about the 11-year-old girl who conceived a child with a 15-year-old boy is most relevant in this respect. In this story we see a myriad of factors and behaviours associated with the underclass. Put together in this way, they create a toxic mix for the reader. First, there is alcohol abuse (the girl's baby is conceived during a drunken night out). Then, precocious sexual behaviour, coupled with ignorance of an extreme kind (the girl did not think that, as a virgin, she could become pregnant; her seemingly naive assertions about being 'able to cope' with motherhood). The story also contains elements of criminality and antisocial behaviour (the father of the unborn baby has been charged with rape; the girl has been excluded from school). The mother-to-be also engages in poor health behaviours and disregard for the well-being of her child (she smokes 20 cigarettes a day). Moreover, she holds age-inappropriate motivations (she says she is 'looking forward to being a mum'). And we see also the cultural entrenchment of such behaviour and its intergenerational transmission (the girl's mother is 'proud' of her daughter; the girl has had 'lots of practice looking after' her brothers, suggesting that she comes from a large family and one where the young grandmother-to-be's own child bearing began at an early age).

Diverting though this story is, in respect of maternal age at least, it is certainly not a tale that is typical of either most 12-year-olds or most teenage mothers. Of the 101,900 conceptions to females aged under 20 in England and Wales in 2005, 59,701 (nearly 60%) were to women aged 18 or 19. In the same year, there were 327 girls aged under 14[4] who became pregnant, generating an under-14 conception rate of 1 per 1,000. Of these, just 132 continued with the pregnancy (ONS, 2005). The statistical oddity of pregnancy at such a young age is not noted in the newspaper reports, where there is an absence (other than the ages of the protagonists) of numbers or other 'evidence' about teenage pregnancy.

These stories about teenage pregnancy – that it is an epidemic, that it is symbolic of the underclass – are typified in the 'Teenage pregnancy as calamity' discourse. Journalists also sometimes make use of photographic images – though there are fewer images of teenage mothers in the press than there are words about them – and, where images are used, they immediately signal 'teenage mother' to the reader. Often, the young mothers in photographs that accompany the text are wan faced and pale. Sometimes they are overweight and slovenly looking. They are shown pregnant, or carrying babies or, more sinisterly, teddy bears or dolls. Teenage mothers nearly always look as if they are in despair. If their neighbourhoods are shown, these are invariably urban and 'gritty'. Young mothers may be shown pushing prams, sometimes in the company of other teenage mothers, suggesting that teenage motherhood is commonplace in their neighbourhoods.

Although not frequently used, these kinds of image, especially when used with sweeping, emotive language and alarming statistics, exert a powerful effect on the reader. In this way, teenage pregnancy comes to be conveyed as one of society's most urgent problems, and teenage mothers become the modern symbols of doom and despair, signifiers for all that is wrong in contemporary society.

Not letting facts get in the way of a good story

The process of unpacking the ways in which everyday depictions of teenage pregnancy and teenage mothers are created is a fascinating one, and tells us much about the ways in which social problems are created or intensified. Hilgartner and Bosk's observation (paraphrasing the founding father of symbolic interactionism, Blumer) that 'social problems are projections of collective sentiments rather than simple mirrors of objective conditions in society' (1988, pp 53–4) is true of teenage pregnancy, as well as of myriad other 'problems'.

There are two additional points that should be made here in relation to representations of teenage pregnancy in the media. First, because a social issue can be seen as being constructed as a significant problem in the media, it does not mean that the 'objective conditions' referred to by Hilgartner and Bosk above do not pertain. It is possible that social problems come to be designated as such because their objective conditions *are* problematic, but that these conditions are intensified and massively distorted in the process by key players. Teenage pregnancy may or may not be a problem, but the representation of it can be distorted nonetheless. This idea is discussed later in this book. Second, the depiction of teenage pregnancy as problematic is largely the media's making and owes much to the fact that the media deal with caricatures. Academics and policy makers may contribute, inadvertently or otherwise, to the production of negative discourses about pregnant or parenting teenagers, but both generally avoid the kind of language used by journalists and would claim not to give credence to the sentiments that lie behind it.

Ultimately, the myth–reality gap on teenage pregnancy matters: young mothers are aware that they are the objects of policy scrutiny and public opprobrium (Kirkman et al, 2001). They report hostile treatment at the hands of others in their communities and wider society (Arai, 2004; Harden et al, 2006), and are reluctant to use mainstream services, for fear of being judged or ostracised (de Jonge, 2001; Billings and Macvarish, 2007). It is against this backdrop that we should ask: 'Do these stories about teenage pregnancy and motherhood reflect the reality?' and 'Are they accurate and fair?' In some respects, it might be considered not to matter much: the media do not let facts get in the way of a good story and many groups are maligned in the press, and this is something we have to tolerate in a free society. In fact, some teenage mothers may identify with the 'Beating the odds' discourse; it may resonate with them in relation to their life experiences. But many more would, no doubt, baulk at their depiction as omens of calamity. Whatever their veracity, both discourses say a great deal about the kinds of stories told about pregnant and parenting teenagers, and have about them something of the plot of a film or novel ('Teenage pregnancy as calamity' has a sense of the apocalypse about it, with young mothers as the symbols of despair, chaos and disorder). For most people, these are the only stories they are ever told about pregnant and parenting teenagers, and it is not surprising that their understanding of teenage pregnancy is distorted and that they come to regard teenage mothers with hostility.

Summary

Critical consideration of contemporary media representations of pregnant and parenting teenagers requires an awareness not only of the many processes that the journalistic product goes through before it appears on the page or screen, but also of the practice of using research findings in a partial or distorted way. Journalists have a toolbox of stylistic devices at their disposal which seems almost to have been created solely for use when writing about teenage pregnancy and is characterised by the use of hyperbole, metaphors evoking chaos and despair ('floods', 'blight'), repetition of key words and phrases ('kids having kids') and frequent use of adjectives signalling alarm ('rising', 'soaring'). These words and phrases, with or without corroborating statistical data or research findings, together create a powerful picture of pregnant and parenting teenagers. It is a picture that is sometimes mixed (teenage mothers can be 'beautiful' as well as 'pasty-faced', they can even be 'good' mothers occasionally), but the story is nearly always, ultimately, a bleak one. Teenage pregnancy is always, and must always be, a problem.

Notes

[1] http://www.dailymail.co.uk/news/article-1027672/Abortions-14-girls-soared-21-cent.html.

[2] http://news.bbc.co.uk/1/hi/special_report/1999/04/99/teen_pregnancy/329881.stm.

[3] © Telegraph Media Group Limited 2006.

[4] Data on the exact ages of girls aged under 14 who become pregnant are not available.

FOUR

New Labour, a new approach to teenage pregnancy

Introduction

The election of the New Labour government in a landslide victory in 1997 marked the end of nearly two decades of Conservative rule. The party was voted into power again in 2001. In May 2005, Labour achieved a historical party first: its third consecutive term in office.

Early in its first term, the New Labour government made a reduction in teenage pregnancy one of the foci of its reforming policy programme (Evans, 2006). The previous Conservative administration had also attempted to reduce early conceptions, but New Labour's approach was different. The government made a conscious break with previous political stances on teenage pregnancy (and earlier representations of young mothers), which were now deemed to be judgemental. Instead, New Labour sought to recast youthful pregnancy not as a problem of sexual morality but as a cause, and consequence, of health and socioeconomic inequalities.

This idea was articulated at length in the government's seminal policy report on the issue: *Teenage Pregnancy* (SEU, 1999). The report described trends in teenage pregnancy and fertility, made comparisons with rates in other countries, offered explanations for early pregnancy (drawing on the large body of research in this area) and introduced the long-term, multifaceted campaign to reduce it: the Teenage Pregnancy Strategy (TPS) and the unit (the TPU) that would house the strategy. The TPS has two main targets: to halve the under-18 conception rate by 2010 and establish a downward trend in the under-16 rate; and to increase the numbers of teenage parents in education, training or employment to 60% by 2010, to reduce their risk of social exclusion.

It is the reframing of the 'problem' of teenage pregnancy and motherhood, the ways in which representations of pregnant and mothering teenagers differed under New Labour, the run-up and reaction to *Teenage Pregnancy* and the TPS and the kind of explanations for (and solutions to) teenage pregnancy offered within it, and how these reflect New Labour philosophy, that are considered in this chapter. The first target of the TPS, to reduce conception rates, has always been, arguably, the more difficult to attain as well as the more politically contentious, and is the principal focus here. From the time of the introduction of the TPS, and to this day, there continues to be an often-acrimonious debate about how this might be achieved: through access to sex education, greater provision of contraception, or the withdrawal of welfare benefits and social housing to young mothers, or even through some kind of moral 'reawakening' among young people. Some of these debates are touched on here.

The TPS came into existence in 1999 and is an ongoing strategy, one which may continue in some form beyond 2010, so this chapter has been written with an eye both to the recent past and to the near future. However, the focus here is on the first few years of the life of the TPS – when New Labour really was 'New' and teenage pregnancy was high on the policy agenda and in the public consciousness, and the subject of excited media coverage.

Policy on teenage pregnancy before New Labour

As North American academics have observed, at some point in the late 1960s/early 1970s the stigma previously attached to out-of-wedlock child bearing shifted to teenage pregnancy and motherhood (Arney and Bergen, 1984; Wong, 1997; Vinovskis, 2003). This change also occurred in the UK and was probably related to the growth in cohabitation that occurred around this time. It was easy to condemn child bearing outside marriage when a small proportion of the population engaged in it, but was more difficult when cohabitation became widespread. The popularity of cohabitation increased such that, by 2006, 44% of births were outside marriage in England and Wales and, of those births registered jointly, 64% were registered by parents living at the same address (ONS, 2007).

Despite this shift in thinking, some confusion remained about which behaviours were socially proscribed, as evidenced by the 'slippage' of categories of people considered problematic (Macintyre and Cunningham-Burley, 1993). In British political speeches of the late 1980s and the 1990s, 'single', 'lone', 'unwed' and 'underage', 'teenage' (or 'young') mothers variously were singled out for opprobrium by politicians of the day, with apparently little realisation that these are all different demographic categories (Selman, 1998/2001; Linne and Jones, 2000).

Political events in the period from the late 1980s to the mid 1990s form a significant backdrop to the exploration of policy on teenage pregnancy in the last years of the old millennium. In both decades, British governments regarded teenage pregnancy as a problem, though for different reasons and remediable by different means. However, it is 1993 – when John Major introduced his 'Back to Basics' campaign, calling for a return to 'traditional morality' – that is the true starting point for the present analysis, because it was this ill-fated venture that (in part) led to the election of a New Labour government in 1997. Doig (2001) links our understanding of the term 'sleaze' with 'the revelations that played a significant role in the collapse of confidence in the Major government and its subsequent defeat in 1997' (p 360). These 'revelations' will not be described here except to say that, very much against the spirit of 'Back to Basics', they largely involved sexual shenanigans among Tory politicians.

Throughout the 1980s and early 1990s, politicians from the Conservative party repeatedly highlighted the role played by single and/or young mothers in the erosion of 'traditional' values and the consequent destabilisation of society. A number of political speeches or other events from this time have come to symbolise this period of political history. One of the most notorious was Peter Lilley's speech to his party in 1992. His remaking of the Gilbert and Sullivan classic 'I've got a little list' ('Young ladies who get pregnant just to jump the housing list. And dads who won't support the kids of ladies they have ... kissed') attracted excited press attention at the time and is still remembered more than 15 years later.[1] Similarly, his colleague John Redwood provoked a 'storm of protest' when he suggested that teenage single mothers should have their babies adopted and that they were given preferential treatment on the housing waiting list:

> 'If no one in the family can help, maybe the girl should consider letting a couple adopt her child to provide the home the baby needs.' The former Welsh Secretary ... also said that young women with illegitimate children were jumping the housing queue. (*Sunday Mirror*, 13 August 1995)

John Major's 'Back to Basics' campaign was significant not only because it was pivotal in leading to the downfall of the Tories in 1997, but also because it positioned young, single mothers – in the starkest and most brutal way – as the enemies of decent society. Daguerre (2006) observes that the Tories' approach to teenage pregnancy and motherhood can be described by the paradoxical combination of an 'aggressive rhetoric regarding young mothers and the absence of any significant policy initiatives in this area' (p 68).

Importantly, though, an initiative had been introduced under the Tories to reduce teenage conceptions. One of the targets of the Health of the Nation (HOTN) strategy was a reduction in pregnancies to girls under 16. HOTN was a five-year strategy running from 1992 to 1997 and represented the first explicit attempt by government to improve the overall health of the whole population (DH, 1998). The evaluation of HOTN suggested that the strategy was largely ineffective, having failed to meet many of its targets. Certainly there was little substantial change in under-16s conceptions (Mayor, 1998). The 1989 baseline rate used in HOTN for girls aged under 16 (13–15) was 9.5 conceptions per 1,000. This figure decreased from 1989 to 1993, dropping to 8 per 1,000, but the 1994 figures showed an upturn in the rates to 8.2 (Adler, 1997). The HOTN target was 4.8, to be achieved by the year 2000. In fact, by that year, and in the third year of New Labour's first term in office, the conception rate for girls aged under 16 was 8.3 per 1,000 (ONS, 2005), a mere 13% decline from the 1989 figure.

The run-up to Teenage Pregnancy

Teenage pregnancy and parenthood have featured regularly throughout New Labour's time in office. The party had shown interest in reducing youthful reproduction before the 1997 election and, when Labour came to power, the government expressed a commitment to addressing the pressing issues of social exclusion and inequalities in health, and to being 'evidence-based' in its approach to dealing with these problems.

In March 1998 the government released the consultation document *Reducing the rates of teenage conception: Towards a national programme*, and set up an advisory group on teenage pregnancy. Tony Blair asked the Social Exclusion Unit (SEU), created just a few months previously in December 1997, to develop a package of reforms to help socially excluded groups, including teenagers at risk of pregnancy and teenage parents. There was a delay in the publication of *Teenage Pregnancy* and its release date was changed several times. This intensified speculation about what the strategy might look like and whether it could placate warring factions such as 'family values' campaigners (who generally oppose sex education) and young people's sexual health advocates, keen to promote greater use of contraception. There was a flurry of sensational articles about teenage sexuality in the media in the weeks and months before the release of *Teenage Pregnancy*. In February 1998, for example, a prominent reproductive health doctor was accused of the 'chemical castration' of children after he suggested that contraceptive implants could be inserted in teenage girls as a matter of 'social policy' in areas of high teenage pregnancies (Boseley, 1999). A plan for school nurses to encourage sexually active girls to go on the Pill met with a similar reception (Smithers, 1999).

However sensational the speculation about the proposed new policy on teenage pregnancy, government ministers proceeded carefully, apparently anxious not to make the same mistakes as their Conservative predecessors. The prime minister publicly and repeatedly condemned the Tories' approach to teenage pregnancy, which, he considered, had attacked teenage mothers but ignored 'the damage [pregnancy] does to the education, employment and life chances of young women and girls'. It is hardly surprising that New Labour wanted to speak about teenage pregnancy with a different voice. The Tories had fared badly in relation to matters of adolescent reproductive health. Their campaign for sexual morality had been derailed by the sexual behaviour of party members and HOTN targets in relation to teenage conceptions had not been achieved.

However, while New Labour's approach to teenage pregnancy is widely recognised as being less moralistic than that of previous governments, some of the old, discredited Tory attitudes persisted, albeit disguised in new 'clothes' – the more palatable language of social exclusion (Hoggart, 2003). Under New Labour, teenage pregnancy was strongly linked to social inequalities, not to personal morality, but the association of teenage pregnancy with 'calamity' and social ills remained a central feature of the new government's approach to teenage pregnancy. In his speech to the Labour Party's Annual Conference in Brighton in 1997, Prime Minister Tony Blair spoke about:

> 100,000 teenage pregnancies every year. Elderly parents with whom families cannot cope. Children growing up without role models they can respect and learn from. More and deeper poverty. More crime. More truancy. More neglect of educational opportunities. And above all more unhappiness.[2]

The juxtaposition of teenage pregnancy with social problems (poverty, crime and truancy) was discussed in Chapter Three. From a policy perspective, these phenomena were considered to be, if not one and the same, linked in some way and emblematic of personal despair and social chaos. In this respect, New Labour politicians were little different to their predecessors in their representations of youthful pregnancy.

Later in the same year, Tessa Jowell, a prominent minister, announced an 'action plan' on teenage pregnancy. Echoing her leader's sentiments, she said that:

> An unintended pregnancy can be a disaster for a woman. Getting pregnant as a teenager can be even more of a personal tragedy…. It can affect a girl's education, her relationships with her friends and family. It can mean the end of her education and close doors to her future … Teenage conceptions tend to be both a symptom and a cause of social inequality. They can become part of a cycle of deprivation.[3]

Teenage pregnancy, while a 'disaster' and a 'tragedy' that prevents advancement (in education, in one's personal life), has its roots in social inequality and the 'cycle of deprivation'. Neither personal morality nor even sexual behaviour was mentioned by Jowell, as they might have been if a politician from the previous administration had made the speech.

Though more temperate in their use of language, and keen to associate the cause of teenage pregnancy with social exclusion rather than with morality, not only did Labour politicians do as their predecessors had done and associate teenage pregnancy with social ills, they also confused quite discrete social issues. Like John Redwood before him, Jack Straw attracted criticism when he apparently advocated the greater use of adoption of babies born to teenage mothers:

> Jack Straw, the Home Secretary, was last night at the centre of a political storm after he said that more teenage mothers should surrender their children for adoption … Mr Straw said: 'It is in no-one's interests … to allow a situation to develop whereby a crisis point is reached in the baby's first year because the ability of the mother, often a teenage mother, to cope has been misjudged' … Mr Straw said he was surprised that in 1997 there were more than 3,500 children under two being looked after by local authorities, while couples wanting to adopt had to wait for years … Mr Straw said teenage mothers offering their children for adoption could result in a better life for the baby. (*Guardian*, 26 January 1999)

Jack Straw appeared to make these statements based on the assumption that those babies left languishing in the care system were most likely to be the children of teenage mothers (though we are presented with no evidence that they are). In addition, the problems associated with the adoption system, which may be genuine and warrant reform, were confused with teenage pregnancy and motherhood, though these were, and continue to be, quite separate issues.

Teenage Pregnancy **and its meanings**

Speculation about the government's policy ended on 14 June 1999, when *Teenage Pregnancy* was published. Tony Blair, drawing on the main themes of the report, wrote a piece for the *Daily Mail* outlining his plans. The Prime Minister seemed to have had younger teenagers in mind, speaking as he did about his belief that, in a 'civilised society', children should not be having children. He expressed his view that young people should not have sex before they are 16 ('but, if they do, they need to avoid the very real risks that underage sex brings'). And, tapping into earlier debates about the role of welfare benefits in teenage pregnancy, the Prime Minister asserted that he did not 'believe leaving a 16-year-old girl with a baby in her own flat, often halfway up a tower block, benefits her, the baby or the rest of us'. He concluded by saying that:

> I know teenage pregnancy is a difficult and politically sensitive issue. It's hardly surprising that past Governments have shied away from tackling it. But that neglect has meant ... far too many un-planned, unwanted pregnancies and young lives blighted by poverty and shattered dreams. (*Daily Mail*, 14 June 1999)

As if to justify this high-profile policy interest, later the same year, there were a couple of spectacular (and highly atypical) examples of very young teenage pregnancy. In Rotherham, a 26-year-old mother discovered her 12-year-old daughter was pregnant. The child had conceived when she was just 11 (Wainwright, 1999). In nearby Sheffield, another 12-year-old became pregnant by her 14-year-old boyfriend (Brown, 1999). Predictably perhaps, both cases were cited as examples of moral and societal decay, and media commentary on the cases meshed with observations about the government's new policy on teenage pregnancy for many weeks and months.

Teenage Pregnancy is an interesting document and one worthy of analysis for a number of reasons, but there are three features of it that stand out as immediately significant, and they will be discussed here in detail. These features of *Teenage Pregnancy* – illustrative of the ways in which youthful reproduction was described, conceptualised and addressed as a problem under New Labour – are focused on: its philosophy (*Teenage Pregnancy* reflected New Labour philosophy, especially in the report's focus on a 'third way' on teenage pregnancy); the kinds of explanation for youthful pregnancy that it offered (which were accepted at the time and quickly entered the mainstream); and its use of statistical 'evidence' to describe teenage pregnancy (its epidemiology, correlates and consequences), and the absence of other kinds of evidence, especially that of a qualitative nature. Each of these is considered below.

Teenage Pregnancy *and New Labour philosophy*

Teenage Pregnancy strongly embodied, and reflected, New Labour political thought. There has been a lot written about New Labour's place in British political history and the party's philosophy. It is beyond the scope of this book to explore this in detail, except to say that much of this discussion centres on the differences between the mid/late 1990s incarnation of the party and its earlier versions (what, therefore, makes it 'New' and not 'Old' Labour). Here, two major expressions of this difference are considered important to an understanding of New Labour's approach to teenage pregnancy. The first of these is New Labour's espousal of a 'third way' in politics. The third way has been defined as being:

> based on a characterization of two previous political 'ways': the socialism/social democracy of the 'old left' (first way) and the free-market neoliberalism of the new right (second way). It seeks to adopt what it sees as the strengths of these traditions, while avoiding their weaknesses....The Third Way thus refuses what it sees as the false political binaries of the past ... arguing that they are reconcilable ... (Leggett, 2007)

The third way is, as this definition makes clear, about a synthesis of old and new in an effort to *modernise* the political process. Labour's modernising agenda, and reference to the modernising process in the use of language by New Labour politicians, has been written about by many commentators. Newman (2001) observes that:

> The Third Way attempted to forge a new political statement by drawing selectively on fragments and components of the old, and reconfiguring these through the prism of a *modernised* economy, a *modern* public service and a *modern* people. (p 46, emphasis added)

The second way in which New Labour differed from previous incarnations is in its focus on reducing health and socioeconomic inequalities. Of course, this was not a novel idea, or one taken up solely by Labour, but it was the linkage of this to the concept of 'social exclusion' that is significant here. Social exclusion is a complex idea on which there is a voluminous literature. Its modern origins lie in French political thought (Todman, 2004), and it has been analysed prolifically by Levitas (1998) and widely critiqued. There is no accepted definition of social exclusion; however, the SEU (2004) describes it as:

> a shorthand term for what can happen when people or areas suffer from a combination of linked problems such as unemployment, discrimination, poor skills, low incomes, poor housing, high crime, bad health and family breakdown. (p 3)

Social exclusion is, therefore, about more than simple, class-based inequalities, and, importantly, it can have a spatial element: certain kinds of phenomena (unemployment, poor health) are features of some places rather than of others, thus marking out individuals and communities as 'excluded'.

Social exclusion, with its focus on multifaceted and multidimensional exclusion from the mainstream among some individuals or communities, and the third way, a new way of 'doing' politics that emphasises a rejection of the binaries of the past and instead advocates a resynthesis of ideas in an effort to modernise the political process, were key themes in *Teenage Pregnancy* and the TPS, the strategy outlined within it (Bullen et al, 2000). Social exclusion was an obvious theme running throughout *Teenage Pregnancy*: teenage pregnancy is considered to be both a cause and consequence of it. A third way on teenage pregnancy is not referred to, but is implicit in *Teenage Pregnancy*'s rejection of the past (especially of previous moralistic and ineffective efforts to reduce teenage pregnancy) and its more socially and politically acceptable reframing of the problem and solutions to it in an effort to make the TPS appealing to as many groups as possible.

New Labour's third way on teenage pregnancy – with its rejection of 'old' ideas, especially those espoused by groups with a high-profile interest in youthful sexual behaviour, and its reframing of the problem in a bid to gain wider acceptability – might also be seen as an example of a 'sitting on the fence' approach to policy. This was noted by media commentators at the time of the introduction of the TPS. Polly Toynbee (1999), of the *Guardian*, wrote about the new policy as a 'botched job' and accused the government of sending out 'mixed messages' on sex. Others noted the government's difficulties in finding a third way on teenage pregnancy between 'moralism and practicality': 'the strategy prepared by the Social Exclusion Unit would try to pick its way through the political minefield between strong anti-sex messages for teenagers and more contraception and sex education' (Wintour, 1999).

Explanations for teenage pregnancy

At the heart of *Teenage Pregnancy* three reasons were offered for youthful conception. These were: 'low expectations', 'ignorance' and 'mixed messages' (SEU, 1999, p 7). The first, 'low expectations', offered a structural reason for youthful conception, one related to socioeconomic disadvantage. From this perspective, it was acknowledged that high levels of income inequality in the UK can lead to 'poor expectations' among youth about their chances of educational or vocational success: 'there are more young people who see no prospect of a job … they see no reason not to get pregnant' (p 7). The second reason, 'ignorance', was a consequence of lack of knowledge about contraception, sexual health and the reality of parenthood: teenagers 'do not know how easy it is to get pregnant and how hard it is to be a parent' (p 7). This was, therefore, largely about technical expertise (the obtaining and effective use of contraception) and education or knowledge (about sexual health, the nature of parenthood). The third reason for teenage pregnancy was 'mixed messages'. These were social or cultural in nature: 'One part of the adult world bombards teenagers with sexually explicit messages and an implicit message that sexual activity is the norm. Another part … is at best embarrassed and at worst silent …' (p 7). For the purposes of developing the argument here, these explanations for teenage pregnancy can be (broadly) categorised into three groups: 'structural', 'technical/educational' and 'social/cultural'.

A number of points should be made about these explanations. First, it is not clear which best explained *either* early sexual behaviour *or/and* teenage pregnancy *or/and* fertility. The authors of *Teenage Pregnancy* seemed not to have been sure about this and mentioned 'birth rates' as much as they did 'pregnancy'. To cover any confusion, the observation was simply made that 'individual decisions about *sex* and *parenthood* are never simple to understand' (p 7, emphasis added).

However, *Teenage Pregnancy*'s authors did imply that structural factors ('low expectations') might better explain fertility (unemployment and lack of engagement with education might make unplanned pregnancy less unattractive, since it would not interfere with school or work). Technical/educational factors were considered possibly to have a greater effect on sex and pregnancy, since 'ignorance' about sex and contraception leads to unplanned pregnancy (though these factors were also believed to influence the decision to continue with a pregnancy: knowledge about the 'reality of parenthood' also featured under this explanation). Social/cultural influences on behaviour, since these were seen as largely comprising messages about sex, might also be considered to affect sexual behaviour and pregnancy more than fertility (though they could also apply to decisions about child bearing: early motherhood might be more acceptable in some social contexts as compared to others, for example, and be affected by peer messages about early fertility).

Second, not only was it unclear which factors best explained teenage sex, pregnancy or fertility: these were not mutually exclusive categories and were easily conflated, especially technical/educational and social/cultural categories.

Third, despite the overlap between these three categories, there were inherent tensions between them that were little recognised at the time but that are, in fact, broadly aligned with the ideological fault lines running through the debate on teenage pregnancy. 'Family values' groups, for example, have traditionally emphasised the role of cultural values (social/cultural) on teenage sexual behaviour and pregnancy (see, for example, van Loon, 2003), while sexual health advocates have tended to stress the importance of greater provision of contraception and improved sex education (technical/educational, see, for example, Hadley, 1998).

Teenage Pregnancy's authors were hoping to avoid controversy by accounting for teenage pregnancy with such all-encompassing explanations. However, for many commentators on teenage sexual and reproductive behaviour, there is often little distinction between sexual activity, pregnancy and parenthood; they are often attributed to the same factors. And the fact that these explanations might overlap, or be a point of tension, was also of secondary importance (except for those high-profile groups who publicly emphasised this).

The degree to which any of these categories better explained either early sex, pregnancy or parenthood (or one rather than another) was not of great importance for another reason: all were usually attributed to technical/educational factors (with an implicit understanding that these were informed by social/cultural and structural influences). The dominance of technical/educational explanations may be attributable to a poor understanding of social/cultural influences on behaviour. Or, it may be that these types of explanation – by attributing to young women a degree of ignorance about sex and its consequences – were appealing because ignorance is (relatively) easily remedied by better provision of knowledge and education.

This thinking also suited contemporary beliefs about the transformative power of education, and reflected the spirit of the age. Technical/educational explanations of teenage pregnancy became fashionable in an era in which safe, effective contraception had been developed, and the belief prevailed that human reproduction could be controlled. Luker (1996) reiterates this when she says that, by the 1970s, 'unwanted or untimely pregnancies came to be viewed as technological failures' (p 51). Similarly, Arney and Bergen (1984) observe that, from 1970 on, teenage mothers became a 'technical' problem and educational intervention was required: 'The proximate cause of pregnancy was an "appalling ignorance" about the true nature of sexuality' (p 15). Geronimus (1997) notes that 'family planners' acknowledge the connection between teenage pregnancy and poverty, but they also see it as 'an educational or medical problem to be solved by increased access to contraception, abortion and sex education' (p 3). In Carabine's (2007) analysis of the TPS, the 'acquisition of knowledge' and its deployment to prevent pregnancy is flagged up as one of the most significant elements of the TPS.

Technical/educational explanations for (and solutions to) teenage pregnancy clearly have a relatively long history, one that coincides with the history of the problematisation of teenage pregnancy. One of their major limitations is that they stifle understanding of other kinds of explanations for teenage pregnancy, or other ways of seeing teenage parenthood. In particular, the dominance of technical/educational explanations marginalises social/cultural explanations – little research has been conducted, for example, on the reasons for the apparent opposition to abortion in the poorest communities, or the extent to which early motherhood in some social contexts may reflect a genuine desire for early parenthood (Tabberer et al, 2000; Bell et al, 2004).

Technical/educational approaches continue to be attractive to policy makers for another significant reason: interventions to reduce teenage pregnancy that are based on the provision of information or education are also relatively cheap. Women in the unskilled, manual social classes are 10 times more likely to become young mothers than their counterparts from professional-class backgrounds (Botting et al, 1998), and early pregnancy and child bearing is concentrated in the poorest neighbourhoods (and abortion in the most affluent) (Smith, 1993), yet the reduction of deprivation is seldom suggested as the *principal* means of reducing teenage pregnancy (Luker, 1996).

The tone of the 1999 report, and the recommendations made (based on findings from 70 projects concerned with provision of sex education and/or information about contraception), suggested that technical/educational explanations for early pregnancy were paramount in policy approaches. The Health Education Board for Scotland (Burtney, 2000) drew on the same research as the SEU in its report on teenage pregnancy. In this document, there was little reference to the effect of structural factors on teenage pregnancy, although the author did accept that there are links between teenage parenthood and poverty and that reducing 'inequalities in life circumstances' would reduce inequalities in unwanted teenage pregnancy (Section 4).

Types of evidence

The third feature of *Teenage Pregnancy* that merits further consideration is its use of 'evidence'. The research cited was primarily that reporting the analysis of statistical data. Many analyses of this kind have found negative outcomes for early motherhood, and it was these that were primarily used as 'evidence' to justify intervening to reduce early pregnancy (Graham and McDermott, 2005; Wilson and Huntington, 2006). The apparently 'evidence-based' approach of *Teenage Pregnancy* gave the report a validity that it might not have merited, and obscured the fact that it was a policy output, and not an impartial document.

There were many quotes scattered throughout *Teenage Pregnancy*, but it is not clear how they were generated or to what kind of analysis (if any) they were subjected. Where these quotes were used, they contributed to the perception of teenage pregnancy as the bleakest of events. Consider these extracts, where pregnant adolescents report hostile reaction to news of their pregnancy. The quotes depict a picture of harsh parental rejection of the mother-to-be, and are reminiscent of the treatment of pregnant young women in an earlier historical period.

I've just found out I'm pregnant. My mum gave me three days to decide on an abortion. When I told her I wanted to keep it, she threw me out. But I want to go back home. I miss her.

My dad threw my sister out when she got pregnant. He's hit her before. I'm so scared I think I'm going to run away.

I'm 15 tomorrow. I'm pregnant. The doctor told me I should have an abortion. My mum told me to get out and let social services put me in care. I just want to go home. (SEU 1999, p 55)

The ways in which qualitative data were used in *Teenage Pregnancy*, as well as the lack of reference to examples of methodologically robust qualitative research, left us with a highly partial understanding of young women's experience of pregnancy and parenthood and served to underscore the perception of youthful pregnancy as the most tragic of events.

These three features of *Teenage Pregnancy* have been described here as typifying the New Labour approach to early conception and fertility. In summary, *Teenage Pregnancy*'s grounding in third way philosophy can be seen as a demonstrable rejection of past approaches to teenage pregnancy and as an attempt to reconcile competing interest groups. The kinds of explanations offered for teenage pregnancy, which were all-encompassing, were emblematic of this, though the supremacy of explanations based on provision of knowledge and information reflected both the spirit of the age (that information can solve everything) and cost constraints. *Teenage Pregnancy*'s use of statistical 'evidence', and the relative omission of other kinds of evidence, bolstered the perception of early fertility as a wholly negative phenomenon, and also gave the report legitimacy.

The TPS and its fortunes over a decade

Effectiveness of the TPS

From 1999 to the present day, the TPU implemented the TPS (as well as commissioning new research to inform it). It was regularly evaluated during that time and considered to be making progress toward its targets (Wellings et al, 2005). There has been a reduction in teenage conception rates during this period, but the TPS is unlikely to meet its 2010 targets in relation to a halving of under-18 conception rates, despite positive evaluation in other areas.

Over a decade of implementation, the strategies used by the TPU have changed as rates remained resistant to change (or the degree of change required) and the hoped-for reduction could not be attained. It may be that these targets were unrealistic in the first place and could never have been achieved in a decade. Or it may be that the TPS is not appropriate for some areas, or has been unevenly implemented. No doubt, there will be many explanations for the TPS's (relative) failure on reductions in rates. Considering the fortunes of the TPS over the decade, there is an increasing sense of policy makers 'flailing around', with the TPU ultimately looking to others to help it bring about a reduction in rates and, at one point, asking parents to intervene to do more. The media were quick to pick up on this as a sign of desperation:

> The government has reached the limits of its ability to contain the UK's high rate of teenage pregnancy and can go no further without the help of parents ... Beverley Hughes [said] ... that ministers had 'reached a sticking point' where their efforts could not by themselves solve the problem of teenage pregnancy ... Ms Hughes insisted that the government ... had 'done all the right things' ... But she added: 'I don't think there is any magic bullet ... that we can identify that is going to now take another substantial step forward'. (*Guardian*, 26 May 2005)

The TPU pioneered the idea of 'hotspots', areas where teenage pregnancy rates remain high, and published *Teenage pregnancy: Accelerating the strategy to 2010* (DfES, 2006) to provide a 'boost' to the implementation of the TPS. In this document, changes in local rates, and possible reasons for them, were explored at length. Using the language of epidemiology, the authors describe 'correlations' and carefully 'targeted interventions'. But, however scientific the language, the authors cannot hide the fact that changes in rates cannot be properly accounted for. There is a clear attempt in the report not to appear to be apportioning blame, but a barely concealed 'naming and shaming' of areas runs through it:

> All Local Authorities and PCTs have under 18 conception rate targets which they are expected to reach by 2010 to meet the national PSA reduction of 50%. Some are making

> excellent progress, while others are performing badly. (DfES, 2006, p 14)

One of those performing badly was Manchester, which had experienced a 14.4% *increase* in its under-18 conception rate by 2005 (Manchester PCT Board Meeting, 3 October 2007). In London, the City of Westminster, on the other hand, experienced a significant decline in teenage conception rates, almost reaching its targeted 50% reduction three years before 2010.[4]

While factors affecting teenage pregnancy (poor educational attainment, low aspirations) were flagged up in *Accelerating the strategy*, we are led to believe that the reasons for variations in conception rates lie primarily in variation in the implementation of the TPS, and not in features of the local areas or populations. Instead, the TPU referred to the work of local 'champions', provision of sexual health education and active youth services as key to reductions in rates and observed that:

> High performing areas have demonstrated that if the strategy is implemented effectively and with strong commitment, teenage conception rates can fall very substantially. It is therefore neither inevitable nor acceptable that rates should be static or rising in other areas. (p 15)

This explanation for variation in rate decreases was reiterated in February 2009, when release of the 2007 conception rates showed an increase in pregnancy rates among both under-18s and under-16s. *The Times* declared the TPS to be a policy 'disaster' and noted that the government had responded by declaring a £20.5m package to promote contraception (Bennett, 2009).

Summary

In summary, New Labour's approach to teenage pregnancy can be characterised as a rejection of the moralistic condemnation of pregnant and parenting teenagers that was espoused by politicians and others in the 1980s and early 1990s, and a reframing of the 'problem' as one linked to social exclusion. Seen this way, early pregnancy was believed to be a consequence of external factors, such as lack of opportunity and confused messages about sex, rather than a personal moral deficit. Some understanding of political events in the years preceding the party's election to power in 1997 is warranted in order to contextualise the government's apparently distinctive approach to teenage pregnancy.

Teenage Pregnancy, the seminal policy document that introduced the TPS, reflected and embodied New Labour philosophy, with its focus on finding a third way on teenage pregnancy and its recognition of the deleterious effects of social exclusion on the lives of individuals and communities. Despite offering three types of explanation for youthful pregnancy, 'technical/educational' approaches to teenage pregnancy were paramount in the TPS. That is, the provision of information and (sex) education was advocated as the most likely means by which a reduction in conception rates might be attained. *Teenage Pregnancy* relied on the use of statistical studies on teenage pregnancy and made little reference to qualitative work, especially that on young women's own experience of motherhood. This reinforced the idea of early pregnancy as having entirely negative consequences and gave the report an 'evidence-based' validity. Conception rates have declined since the late 1990s, though there was a rise in the 2007 figures, but the 2010 target will probably be missed, although the strategy is ongoing and a full evaluation is forthcoming.

Notes

[1] http://news.bbc.co.uk/1/hi/programmes/the_daily_politics/6967366.stm

[2] www.prnewswire.co.uk/cgi/news/release?id=47983

[3] http://www.gov-news.org/gov/uk/news/action_plan_on_teenage_pregnancy_announced/326.html

[4] www.westminster-pct.nhs.uk/news/teenage_pregnancy.htm

Part Two
Unmaking a problem

FIVE

What are the consequences of teenage fertility?

Introduction

In the academic and policy literature, teenage pregnancy is sometimes *assumed* to be a problem, with little or no effort expended on explaining why it is considered so (Macintyre and Cunningham-Burley, 1993). In the same way that phenomena such as crime, homelessness and drug addiction are avowedly negative, teenage pregnancy is often held to be (in and of itself) a problem (Breheny and Stephens, 2007a). The fact that teenage pregnancy is so often referred to alongside crime, drugs and so on as if these were all part of the same thing, confirms this and reinforces the association between early conception and all kinds of social ills.

Where authors have justified their concern with teenage pregnancy, they usually point to its having consequences in two main areas. Daguerre and Nativel (2006) usefully describe four broad reasons why teenage pregnancy is considered problematic within policy discourses: teenagers are too young (biologically and socially) to bring up children; they lack the maturity needed to make informed decisions about sex; early motherhood causes poverty; and teenagers are financially dependent. These four could be condensed into two, even broader, categories: the alleged immaturity of teenagers (which has biological, emotional and social dimensions and impacts on sexual and parenting behaviours and reproductive outcomes); and teenagers' economic dependency on others (which will likely be exacerbated by early child bearing). From this perspective, teenage pregnancy is *both* a socioeconomic problem *and* a (very broadly defined) health-related one. The socioeconomic consequences of early motherhood, which are focused on poverty and employment prospects, also touch on educational attainment and partnership behaviour, since these impact on poverty (lack of educational attainment leads to reduced job prospects, lone parents are poorer than couples). The health-related consequences are believed to relate to birth outcomes, maternal health, poor sexual health and, very importantly, the shorter- and longer-term impact on the children of teenage mothers, especially in terms of their physical and emotional development. These diverse outcomes of early child bearing are reflected in a large body of literature which straddles different disciplines.

When the TPS was presented to the British public in 1999, much was made of the ill effects of teenage motherhood. In relation to both health and socioeconomic consequences, early pregnancy was described as leading inexorably to social exclusion. In *Teenage Pregnancy*, a number of analyses of large-scale statistical data which found negative outcomes for early motherhood were drawn on, and it was (and continues to be) research such as this that was used to bolster the perception of teenage pregnancy as the cause of adverse outcomes. At the time, and reflecting the tendency described above, teenage pregnancy was accepted as problematic with little consideration or debate about whether this was true or not.

Yet, there has been for many years a vigorous debate about the degree to which teenage motherhood 'causes' poor outcomes, either to mothers or to their children. It is a debate that has been conducted mostly by social scientists (especially economists, who undertake elaborate, complex analyses of data in an attempt to isolate the effects of teenage fertility on various outcomes), and by medical or public health academics describing the alleged harmful biological effects of pregnancy and childbirth in a population considered to be physically and emotionally immature.

The focus of this chapter is on describing the diverse literature on the consequences of teenage child bearing. However, before this can be done, two caveats about this body of work should be made.

Exploring the literature: two caveats

The first relates to the methodological difficulties involved in ascertaining the 'true' (that is, independent) impact of age of child bearing on outcomes. Attempting to measure the effect of having a child in adolescence, independent of such powerful factors as socioeconomic status (SES) and educational attainment, is fraught with problems, and innovative methods have been developed to isolate the potentially confounding effect of other factors. Hoffman (1998) provides a succinct (if now dated) overview of the literature and the main issues encountered by researchers working in this area. He focuses, as have many others (e.g. Lawlor and Shaw, 2002), on the differences between correlation and causation, noting that, in relation to teenage mothers, distinguishing the one from the other does make a difference:

This may sound like another dry academic debate about distinguishing causality from correlation, but it has important policy implications. If we want to make a difference in the lives of these young women, we need to know where and when and how we might best intervene ... Even a successful program to curtail teenage pregnancy might not affect most other aspects of an adolescent's life. It would not ... be likely to alter school, neighborhood and family conditions. Would a pregnancy prevention program with those limitations make a difference? The answer depends on whether the apparent negative effects of teenage childbearing reflect causality or just correlation. (Hoffman, 1998, p 236)

The key question for researchers is: would a woman's life chances be significantly different if she delayed child bearing? It has been suggested that, since teenage mothers come from disadvantaged backgrounds and will have severely limited opportunities in life anyway, the age at which they give birth has little impact on later outcomes. Women from poor backgrounds are, therefore, *selected* into early fertility and any adverse effects arising from it are attributable to SES or other factors and not to early motherhood itself. Or, conversely, it might be maintained that early child bearing makes a poor woman's situation demonstrably worse. In this respect, teenage pregnancy has a *direct* effect on outcomes, and the job of policy makers is to introduce measures to deter it on the grounds that this will benefit women and their children.

Hoffman also talks about the different kinds of innovative methods that have been used to control for selection effects, especially factors which are unmeasured and/or unobserved. These may be factors that are not so easily measurable and on which no data are available in the dataset being analysed. Rather than controlling for SES and other variables, researchers seeking to isolate the effect of early fertility have used 'natural' groups with which to compare teenage mothers. The goal of such work is to identify a group of women who are as similar to teenage mothers as possible, so that differences between the two groups can be attributed to early motherhood and not to other factors.

Hoffman describes three of these approaches and the rationale for their use. First, comparisons of outcomes of sisters, one of whom experienced a birth as a teenager and one who did not. This approach is used on the grounds that sisters are likely to have similar backgrounds (in terms of SES, housing, education and so on) and variations in outcomes can be attributed to birth itself. Second, comparison of teenage mothers who had a singleton birth with teenage mothers who had twins. This approach is used in the belief that the difference between having one baby and having two will be similar to that of having none and one. And third, comparison of teenage mothers with teenagers who conceived but miscarried, since miscarriage is a randomly occurring phenomenon and girls who become pregnant are likely to be similar in other respects.

The second caveat relates to who is doing the research. The literature on the consequences of early fertility can appear polarised, with academics in either one camp or the other (with a little grey in the middle). This may reflect the views of the researchers themselves, or of those funding their work, but it does suggest that researchers may sometimes approach their work with a fixed idea about their findings and the implications of those findings. Even where results go in the opposite way to that expected, the standard 'get out' clause is the assertion that methodological difficulties limited the analysis, or that controls for confounding factors were not sufficient. This may be true, of course, but it is also possible that effects cannot be observed because they were not there in the first place, they were so small as to be nearly insignificant, or they were present but the researcher did not fully acknowledge them.

Scope of the review

There is a relatively large and varied body of work on the consequences of teenage parenthood, and it would be impossible to examine it in detail here. To provide the reader with an overview of this material, the focus here is restricted to the consequences of teenage motherhood only (though studies that may have included fathers are discussed), and effects on the mother herself and, to a lesser degree, her children. The literature that is referred to here dates from the late 1990s and includes selected studies from the UK and (to provide a sense of the research undertaken elsewhere) other developed nations. The main results of the review are shown in tabular form, with study details, focus and so on shown, and some information about the steps taken by researchers to minimise the confounding effects of variables such as SES or education.

Socioeconomic research on the outcomes of teenage fertility

Details of selected studies that have explored the impact of teenage motherhood on socioeconomic outcomes (broadly defined) are shown in Table 5.1.

In Table 5.1, brief details of 14 selected, relatively recent research outputs are shown. The geographic settings in which the analysis was undertaken vary (datasets from the UK, US, New Zealand, Australia and South Africa were used in the studies). The foci of the research also vary, with educational attainment, income and partnership behaviour appearing as important outcomes explored in this body of work. Definitions of 'teenage' can vary slightly, as can the methods of controlling for potentially confounding background factors.

The TPU commissioned research on the outcomes of young parenthood (mothers and fathers) which generated a variety of outputs (see Berrington et al, 2005, for details of these). This work did appear to find an independent effect of age at birth on various health and socioeconomic outcomes for mothers, fathers and children. There was little difference between women who had children in their teenage years and those who deferred birth until their early 20s. Both groups had poor outcomes, mostly attributed to the age at which they gave birth. These findings echoed earlier ones by Hobcraft and Kiernan (1999), which also appeared to find negative effects for early fertility.

The research undertaken by Berthoud and colleagues at the Institute for Social and Economic Research (University of Essex) in the early years of the new millennium, using the BCS70 and other datasets (DH and TPS (DfES), 2004), did find negative effects of early fertility but these were not so strong as the investigators thought they might be. Berthoud and colleagues' (2001) work on the consequences of teenage motherhood in different European countries highlights the importance of considering teenage pregnancy within national contexts. Early parenthood is viewed and treated differently in different countries, and this is likely to have an impact on outcomes. In particular, welfare provision for young mothers varies considerably (Nativel and Daguerre, 2006). Data considerations mean that this cross-national comparative work could not sufficiently control for pre-existing, potentially confounding factors. So, while the analysis is useful in examining variation in outcomes across Europe, the degree to which it can be considered to measure the effect of early child bearing on outcomes is limited.

Table 5.1: Consequences of teenage motherhood: selected studies with a socio-economic and related focus, various years and countries

Author(s) and year	Country	Teenage population(s) studied	Outcomes	Dataset(s) used	Main findings	Controls for confounding factors?
Berrington et al (2005)	UK	Women: aged up to 19	Various, including: income; housing tenure; partnership/marriage; health	ALSPAC; BCS70; GHS	Teenage mothers are more likely to suffer disadvantages in adulthood such as poor physical and psychological health. These result largely from mix of predisposing factors and additional consequences of teenage motherhood.	Yes: background factors statistically controlled for.
Berthoud et al (2001)	UK	Women: aged 15–19	Various, including: education; partnership/marriage; employment; income	ECHP; NCDS; BHPS	Comparisons made across several European countries. Teenage mothers are disadvantaged in all countries, but severity varies.	Partial controls used.
Boden et al (2008)	New Zealand	Women: aged up to 21	Various, including: mental health; education; employment	CHDS	No association found between early motherhood and later mental health disorders. Association between early motherhood and later educational achievement and economic circumstances persists after controls.	Yes: controls for SES; family structure etc.
Bradbury (2006)	Australia	Women: aged up to 20	Various, including: education; occupation; partnership/marriage	ALSWH	No evidence for effect of teenage motherhood on education, labour market, income or location. Being a young mother reduces the likelihood of being married in the late 20s. Having a child in the early 20s rather than late 20s leads to greater likelihood of being lone parent.	Yes: data on miscarriages used.

Table 5.1: continued

Author(s) and year	Country	Teenage population(s) studied	Outcomes	Dataset(s) used	Main findings	Controls for confounding factors?
Chevalier and Viitanen (2003)	UK	Women: aged up to 18	Various, including: education; employment	NCDS	Teenage child bearing decreases probability of post-16 schooling by 12% to 24%. Employment experience reduced by up to 3 years and adult pay differential from 5% to 22%.	Yes: background factors statistically controlled for.
DH and TPS (DfES) (2004)	UK	Women: aged up to 20	Various, including: education; employment; income; partner's employment; home ownership; mental health; birth weight	BCS70; BHPS; LFS	Long-term negative consequences of having a teenage birth observed, but these were not as wide-ranging as previously found. Mothers' partners are poorly qualified. Teenage mothers have higher levels of depression in the medium term postpartum.	Yes: data on miscarriages used.
Fletcher and Wolfe (2008)	US	Women: aged up to 19	Various, including: education; income	NLSAH (Add)	Teenage motherhood can lead to large reductions in wages and income and a modest reduction in the probability of graduating from high school. There is little influence on years of schooling and welfare receipt.	Yes: data on miscarriages used.
Francesconi (2008)	UK	Adult children of mothers aged up to 20	Various, including: income; smoking and psychological distress	BHPS	Children born to young mothers (aged 23 or younger) are less successful than children of older mothers. Reduction of early (not just teenage) child bearing will not eradicate child poverty, but does represent one strategy for increasing the life chances of disadvantaged children.	Yes: data on siblings used.

Table 5.1: continued

Author(s) and year	Country	Teenage population(s) studied	Outcomes	Dataset(s) used	Main findings	Controls for confounding factors?
Gustafsson and Worku (2007)	South Africa	Women: aged 18–24	Various, including: education; partnership/marriage; occupation	SAGHS	Teenage child bearing is negatively correlated with completing high school, but most other outcome measures do not show negative effects from teenage motherhood.	Yes: background factors statistically controlled for.
Hobcraft and Kiernan (1999)	UK	Women: aged up to 23	Various, including: maternal health (emotional and physical); receipt of benefits; partnership/marital status	NCDS	There are associations for adult outcomes with age at first birth, even after controlling a range of other childhood background factors.	Yes: background factors statistically controlled for.
Holmlund (2005)	Sweden	Women: aged up to 20	Education	Swedish vital statistics	There is a penalty to teenage motherhood in terms of years of education.	Yes: data on sisters used.
Hotz et al (2005)	US	Women: aged up to 21	Various, including: education; partnership/marital status; income	NLSY	Poor outcomes cannot be attributed to teenage child bearing. Outcomes are the result of social and economic circumstances. Delaying child bearing will not enhance educational attainment or earnings or affect family structure.	Yes: data on miscarriages used.

continued

Table 5.1: continued

Author(s) and year	Country	Teenage population(s) studied	Outcomes	Dataset(s) used	Main findings	Controls for confounding factors?
Kaplan et al (2004)	UK	Women: aged up to 20	Various, including: income; education; partnership/marriage	BCS70	After unobserved heterogeneity is accounted for, large negative effects of teenage child bearing are reduced. Negative effects are not stronger for teenagers falling pregnant before age 18 compared with those who become pregnant aged 18–20. This suggests that negative effects of teenage motherhood are temporary.	Yes: data on miscarriages used.
Klepinger et al (1999)	US	Women: aged up to 20	Various including: labour market participation; income	NLSY	Teenage fertility reduces years of formal education and work experience. It has a significant effect on wages at age 25.	Yes: background factors statistically controlled for.

Francesconi's (2008) paper on adult outcomes for the children of teenage mothers not only contains a brief, useful overview of recent research, but reports the findings of an analysis of British Household Panel Survey (BHPS) data, and focuses on a wide number of outcomes and controls for background effects by using siblings' data. Overall, negative results for early fertility were found, though these affected women up to the age of 23, not just teenage mothers, and the author does emphasise that reduction of teenage pregnancy is only *one* strategy for dealing with child poverty.

In summary, the findings are mixed, and there is no one, strong and consistent message emerging from the research. Where extensive controls (especially where data on miscarriages among teenagers were used) for selection factors into early motherhood have been used by analysts, outcomes for teenage motherhood do not seem to be entirely attributable to the age at which child bearing began. Authors do often report that, though early motherhood can be demonstrated to have deleterious effects, these are not as strong as previously believed.

Health-related research on the outcomes of teenage fertility

Details of studies with a health-related focus (again, very broadly defined) are shown in Table 5.2.

Brief details of 11 studies from various countries, all focusing on the health-related outcomes of teenage motherhood, and for the children of teenage mothers, are shown in Table 5.2.

Because teenagers are considered to be biologically immature (that is, they have not completed the growth to adulthood), pregnancy and child bearing are believed to have adverse health effects for them and their children. Pregnancies are believed to be more difficult (exacerbated by maternal anaemia, smoking and poor nutrition), births more dangerous (with higher rates of premature birth), and infants' health outcomes are worse than for those with older mothers (including higher rates of stillbirth and infants being born small for gestational age). The perceived emotional immaturity of teenagers is often cited as the reason why motherhood would be more difficult for them as compared with older mothers, and their age is given as one explanation for their greater tendency to depression (Cunnington, 2001; Breheny and Stephens, 2007b).

Table 5.2: Consequences of teenage motherhood: selected studies with a health-related focus, various years and countries

Author(s) and year	Country	Teenage population(s) studied	Outcomes	Dataset(s) used	Main findings	Controls for confounding factors?
Chen et al (2007)	US	Women: aged up to 25	Various, including: pre-term delivery; birth weight	Vital statistics	Births to teenage mothers associated with increased risks for pre-term delivery, low birth weight and neonatal mortality.	Yes: controls for race, education, etc.
Cunnington (2001)	Various developed-world countries	Various ages	Various, including: birth weight; anaemia; prematurity	Systematic review	Increased risks of poor outcomes were mostly caused by social, economic, and behavioural factors. Maternal age younger than 16 years was associated with a modest (1.2–2.7 fold) increase in prematurity, low birth weight and neonatal death.	NA
Gueorguieva et al (2001)	US	Children of teenage mothers	Learning disabilities	Vital statistics	Increased risk for educational problems and disabilities among children of teenage mothers is attributed not age but to socio-demographic factors.	Yes: controls for race, education, etc.
Gupta et al (2008)	UK	Women: aged up to 20	Various, including: hypertension; anaemia	CBS	Obstetrics risk of teenage primigravidae is low, except for the risk of pre-term labour. Women aged under 17 years did not have a worse outcome.	No

Table 5.2: continued

Author(s) and year	Country	Teenage population(s) studied	Outcomes	Dataset(s) used	Main findings	Controls for confounding factors?
Jolly et al (2000)	UK	Women: aged up to 34	Various, including: pre-term labour; anaemia; caesarean section rates	Hospital database	Pregnant women aged under 18 years were more likely to deliver pre-term than older women. They had less maternal and perinatal morbidity and were more likely to have normal vaginal deliveries.	Yes: controls for BMI, ethnicity, etc.
Klerman (2006)	Various	Women: aged up to 20 (multiparous)	Various, including: birth weight; pre-term delivery	Literature review	When teenage mothers having second birth are compared with those having first birth, second births have worse outcomes.	NA
López Turley (2003)	US	Children of teenage mothers	Various, including: cognitive development; reading ability; behaviour problems	NSLY	Lower test scores and increased behaviour problems of children born to younger mothers are due not to age but to family background. Maternal age at first birth has a significant effect on test scores, maternal age at the child's birth does not.	Yes: data on siblings used.
Shaw et al (2006)	Australia	Children of teenage mothers: aged 14	Various, including: cognition; self-reports of general health	MUSP	Compared with children of older mothers, children of mothers aged 18 years and under were more likely to have disturbed psychological behaviour, poorer school performance, lower reading ability and were more likely to smoke regularly. Maternal age was not associated with health outcomes.	Yes: controls for SES, smoking, etc.

Table 5.2: continued

Author(s) and year	Country	Teenage population(s) studied	Outcomes	Dataset(s) used	Main findings	Controls for confounding factors?
Smith and Pell (2001)	UK	Women: aged up to 29	Various, including: stillbirth; pre-term delivery	Vital statistics	First teenage births not independently associated with an increased risk of adverse pregnancy outcome. Teenagers are at decreased risk of delivery by emergency caesarean section. Second teenage births associated with threefold risk of pre-term delivery and stillbirth.	Yes: controls for SES, smoking, etc.
Terry-Humen et al (2005)	US	Children of teenage mothers	Various, including: cognition; reading ability; communication	ECLS-K	Controlling for background factors leads to reduction of effect of mother's age on child outcomes, but is still important. Children born to mothers aged 18–19 did not perform better on most measures than children born to mothers aged 17 and under.	Yes: controls for marital status, family structure, etc.
Usta et al (2008)	Beirut	Women: aged up to 30	Various, including: diabetes; pre-eclampsia	Hospital records	Adolescents more likely to deliver pre-term than older women (11.1% vs 5.8%), and suffered more anaemia and pre-eclampsia. In other respects, maternal and perinatal morbidity is comparable.	Yes: controls for parity, health insurance, etc.

Details of a systematic literature review (Cunnington, 2001) are shown in the table. Nearly 6,000 studies were screened in the review. Though only 11 papers were used, they showed that it is largely factors such as poverty and lack of access to services that cause adverse outcomes, and not the age of the mother (except among the youngest teenagers). In relation to one potentially serious birth outcome, premature birth, the author concludes that:

> Before 16 years of age there does appear to be a very real association of teenage pregnancy with prematurity. The very premature babies account for most of the increase in low birth weight and neonatal mortality. The risks associated with young age … are modest compared to those for the social, behavioural and economic risk factors. (p 40)

The point made earlier in relation to the socioeconomic studies can be made here again: there is diversity in findings, which may reflect not only methodological differences (especially in sample populations) but also how robust controls are for background factors that predispose women to early fertility. Cunnington (2001) describes some of these issues and highlights the difficulties of establishing the effect of age on outcomes, given social and behavioural differences among groups of women, with the youngest women at risk of pregnancy the most likely to be living in hazardous social circumstances.

Summary

Teenage pregnancy is depicted as the cause of social exclusion: an event that will severely limit a young woman's life options and have adverse effects on her mental and physical health and that of her children. Other justifications for intervening to reduce teenage pregnancy – that British rates are unacceptably high in the context of lower, Western European rates, for example – are important, but are peripheral, compared with the central association of teenage pregnancy with poor outcomes. It is this association that is repeatedly drawn to attention within initiatives to reduce teenage pregnancy, and the TPS drew attention to the adverse consequences of teenage child bearing in *Teenage Pregnancy* largely using analyses of longitudinal data collected across the life span (e.g. Kiernan, 1997).

Child bearing in the teenage years is considered to cause poor outcomes in two main areas: socioeconomic situation, and health and well-being. There is a long-standing debate about the consequences of early motherhood, and recognition of the conceptual and methodological difficulties of isolating the independent effects of age on outcomes.

Three points can be made in relation to the literature on the outcomes of early fertility. First, looking at the selected studies briefly described here, what is striking about them is that, while many studies do find negative outcomes for teenage mothers, the size of the effects differs so much. This seems to be the case in relation to the health-related outcomes studies and to those focused on socioeconomic outcomes.

Second, the use of longitudinal datasets facilitates the control of pre-existing factors that might predispose to early motherhood, but only those factors that are measured in the dataset can be controlled for. Clearly, factors that might be correlated with teenage motherhood but are unmeasured will therefore be unobservable. Given this, some innovative methods have been developed by researchers exploring the outcomes of teenage motherhood. Comparisons of the life chances of sisters who bore children at different ages, or of young women who experienced birth as teenagers with those who miscarried, provide quasi-natural experimental situations. The use of more sophisticated methodologies to control for selection effects, especially in more recent studies, appears to show reduced effects of early motherhood on outcomes. Hoffman (1998) made a similar point in relation to the US work dating from the 1990s. It would seem, on balance, that even if teenage motherhood has negative effects, these are not as great as policy makers suggest. It is possible, of course, that we will never know the effect of teenage motherhood on outcomes because we cannot measure its effects in isolation from other powerful factors, especially SES.

Third, there may be sufficient doubt to question the basis for the depiction of teenage motherhood as problematic, but policy makers use research to suit their own ends. We are reminded that teenage pregnancy has not always been thought of as problematic and the depiction of teenage pregnancy and motherhood as a problem is relatively new. The association of youthful fertility with poor health and socioeconomic outcomes is the reason typically cited for casting teenage pregnancy as a problem in the UK. In the US, in comparison, it is the association of early fertility with government expenditure on welfare that is considered a more problematic dimension of young motherhood (Rosato, 1999; Bonell, 2004). Whatever the foci of the research, whether on the socioeconomic or health impact of early fertility, no consensus has yet emerged as to whether child bearing in the teenage years actually causes poor outcomes or not.

SIX

Contextualising teenage pregnancy

Introduction

The belief that teenage pregnancy *causes* the poor outcomes that lead to social exclusion has been interrogated by many commentators and there is still no consensus on this. Even where it is accepted that early child bearing might contribute to social exclusion, it appears to have a relatively marginal effect. Given this, the association of teenage pregnancy with social exclusion can seem like a flimsy basis on which to build initiatives such as the Teenage Pregnancy Strategy (TPS).

The reassessment of the effects of early child bearing in Chapter Five, though only an overview, provides some balance to the situation that prevails at present where teenage motherhood is considered to be an event of almost tragic proportions. It also reflects one of the more general aims of this book, to challenge the monolithic assertion that teenage reproduction is always problematic, for young women, their babies and society. This aim is further advanced in this chapter and the next.

The idea of context

In this chapter it is argued that policy, academic and wider social understandings of teenage pregnancy are decontextualised. The idea of something occurring in, or out of, a 'context' is a common enough one. The word's origins lie in the Latin for 'joining together' or 'weaving', which provides a sense of what is commonly understood by 'context'. The concept of 'decontextualised language' – abstract language, removed from its original source – is used by scholars of language and education, especially those interested in young children's acquisition of literacy. One of these, Hamilton-Wieler (1988), in her discussion of texts, provides a useful working definition of decontextualisation, which she defines as: '... the abstraction of a written text or portion of written text from all of its contexts, with the assumption that the isolated text, or portion thereof, is an *autonomous container of its own meaning*' (p 3, emphasis added).

In relation to teenage pregnancy, this definition is apposite. Stripped of context (or of a proper consideration of context), from an examination of the multitude of social, cultural, economic and other factors that influence adolescent sexuality and reproduction, the phrase 'teenage pregnancy' has come, on its own, to embody a set of powerful meanings. In late-20th-century developed societies, these meanings became increasingly negative, to the point where teenage pregnancy is now shorthand for social pathology. If we are to make sense of teenage pregnancy, of the shifting attitudes towards it (over time, over place), and of the discourses surrounding it, it needs to be re-contextualised as an issue. Teenage pregnancy needs to be situated in international, national and local contexts, placed among social and other factors, and understood by reference to them. An exploration of these is the focus of this chapter.

International contexts: comparisons between nations

Cross-national research

The British experience of teenage pregnancy is often located within an international or cross-national context, and there are a number of studies where this has been usefully done (Jones et al, 1986; Wellings and Kane, 1999; Singh and Darroch, 2000; Unicef, 2001; Imamura et al, 2007). Most studies on teenage pregnancy that use cross-national data provide an overview of the situation in a given country, make comparisons with other nations and attempt to delineate broad patterns in behaviour or outcomes. International comparative research is undertaken in many areas of social and health policy and can provide powerful insights into aspects of human behaviour. Berthoud and Iacovou (2002) maintain that comparative (cross-national) research

> is essential. Imagine a world composed of nation-states functioning independently of one another, where scholars and policymakers were only concerned with events within the borders of their own country. Even in this sort of world, researchers should be interested in whether their findings are generalisable to human society as a whole, or to a group of similar countries within the wider world, or whether they are unique to a single country. Even in this sort of a world, we may want to learn from research in another country

> *– but this can only be interpreted properly if the social situation in the other country is understood.* (p 6, emphasis added)

The caveat at the end of this statement has been emphasised because it is this – a proper understanding of 'social situation' – that is absent (or virtually absent) in many of the comparisons made between countries in respect of teenage pregnancy and motherhood. In a British context, the perception of teenage pregnancy as a significant problem is greatly bolstered by comparisons between the UK and other nations, typically Western and Northern European ones. These comparisons are so commonplace that their legitimacy or appropriateness is seldom questioned. It is maintained here that, while comparative research in relation to teenage pregnancy is to be welcomed, many of the comparisons made between the UK and other nations are inappropriate and suffer from a common fallacy about the implementation of interventions: that if something works in one country, then it will work just as effectively in another (Roberts et al, 2006).

The kind of comparison made with other European countries is a familiar one. Some countries (Sweden, Denmark and the Netherlands, in particular) have low teenage fertility. This is believed to be related to a (usually vaguely defined) concept of 'sexual openness' (Jones et al, 1986). The UK could learn by the experience of these nations, particularly in respect of sexual openness and its concomitants, primarily sex education (Hadley, 1998). This argument is built primarily on two assumptions: first, that low Continental teenage fertility rates are a consequence of a low incidence of pregnancy; and second, that (to the relative exclusion of other factors) low teenage pregnancy rates are attributable to the effects of sexual openness and its consequences. These are features of what has already been described as a 'technical/educational' approach to teenage pregnancy, one that emphasises the use of technical (contraceptive) means to avoidance of pregnancy, alongside the acquisition of information.

European experience of teenage pregnancy

The first of these assumptions relates to European pregnancy rates and their variation. This variation is often hidden by judicious presentation of statistical data: conception and abortion rates are presented much less than fertility rates. In part, this is for methodological reasons: data on fertility are more robust than conception and/or abortion data, which, for obvious reasons, are more difficult to collect. Yet, the greater use of fertility data in comparative research also reinforces the perception that the UK performs exceptionally badly in the teenage pregnancy league table. In *Teenage Pregnancy*, data showing teenage (under-20) abortion ratios in various developed-world countries from 1996 were presented. The differences between countries were substantial: Sweden had a teenage abortion ratio of over 1,800 per 1,000 (so, for every 1,000 births to teenagers, there were over 1,800 abortions), Denmark's ratio was about 1,600, while in the UK it was around 600. The authors did not comment on the full implications of these figures (that there is far greater use of abortion in the Scandinavian countries than in the UK), but simply concluded that: 'Given the high level of accidental pregnancies, it is surprising that the UK does not have a higher number of abortions' (SEU, 1999, p 30).

It is not fully appreciated that low teenage fertility rates in some countries are partly attributable to the widespread use of abortion, rather than to a low incidence of conceptions (Unicef, 2001; Ekstrand et al, 2007). This underscores the importance of considering teenage fertility alongside the use of abortion (and paying especial attention to the ratio of abortions to births). In some Scandinavian countries, France and parts of Eastern Europe, high proportions of conceptions to teenagers are aborted. About 40% of conceptions to teenagers in the UK are terminated, as compared with 70% in Sweden. Santow and Bracher (1999) maintain that abortion was more important in the maintenance of low Swedish teenage fertility rates before 1975. Yet, even since the mid-1970s, abortion continues to be important in keeping teenage fertility low in Sweden. In neighbouring Denmark, one survey showed that girls aged 15–19 are almost 40 times more likely to use abortion than women aged 10 years older (Rasch et al, cited in Knudsen and Valle, 2006).

In addition, the existence of relatively large variations in teenage conception rates limits the kinds of generalisations that can be made about the European experience of teenage pregnancy. The UK has the highest youthful conception rates in Western Europe, but comparatively high rates are also found elsewhere in Europe (Iceland, Norway and Sweden, for example), and low rates are present in Italy, the Netherlands and Spain (Singh and Darroch, 2000; Unicef, 2001). These figures also show that low teenage conception rates are a feature of quite different kinds of countries, such as Spain, Italy and the Netherlands. The Netherlands (along with Belgium and Switzerland) has had low teenage pregnancy and fertility rates since the early 1960s. Spain and Italy are among a group of nations where rates of early pregnancy fell in the late 1970s or later (Kane and Wellings, 1999). Little attention is paid to teenage reproductive behaviour in these countries, with the exception of the Netherlands. Spain, Italy (and also Belgium, and the Republic of Ireland, both of which experienced early declines, like the Netherlands) are seldom celebrated for their 'successful' record on teenage pregnancy. From a technical/educational perspective, there appears to be little to link these countries; this might suggest that the reasons for these low rates are varied and complex, and may even be specific to each nation, so few generalisations can be made (Teitler, 2002).

Sexual openness and sex education

The second feature of explanations that use comparisons between the UK and other European nations is the belief that, where teenage conception rates are low, this is because of sexual openness and sex education (Hadley, 1998). Policy on, and provision of, sex education are believed to be affected by social attitudes to sex. A classic study of teenage pregnancy in 35 countries (five in depth) conducted in the 1980s highlighted the central role that sexual openness played in a society's attitude to teenage sexuality (Jones et al, 1986). The UK is believed to perform badly in this regard, and it has become commonplace for commentators to observe that British society's attitude to sex is 'prudish' and that this has an adverse impact on the provision of sex education. Cathy Hamlyn, the former head of the Teenage Pregnancy Unit, publicly derided the UK's 'Benny Hill' attitude to sex and alleged that this is one of the reasons for high teenage pregnancy rates (BBC News Online, 14 July 2002).[1]

There is a large body of literature on sex education, on the different kinds of programmes, methods of evaluation, effectiveness and so on. And there are many different kinds of sex education programme: those embedded within larger programmes compared with stand-alone interventions; school- or community-based initiatives; sex education that promotes abstinence or delay of sexual debut; or programmes aimed at increasing use of contraception. Some programmes seek to increase knowledge or impart sexual negotiation skills to adolescents; others attempt to change sexual or reproductive behaviours.

A full examination of sex education programmes is beyond the scope of this book. There are, however, a number of useful reviews of the effectiveness of sex education interventions. A common problem referred to in this literature (and it is one not confined to evaluation of sex education interventions) is the difficulty of attributing effects to the intervention itself, because of either the poor methodology or variety in the methodology or outcomes, of primary studies. In a systematic review, Oakley and colleagues (1995) demonstrated that, of 73 young people's sexual health interventions, only 12 were methodologically sound enough for inclusion in the review. Of these 12, two showed short-term effects on behaviour.

Another common finding in the literature is that interventions may increase young people's sexual health knowledge, but seldom their behaviour – or, at least, not in any meaningful, long-term and sustainable way. In a meta-analysis of the effectiveness of interventions to reduce repeat pregnancy among teenage mothers (Corcoran and Pillai, 2007), the results showed that at the first follow-up period at which programmes assessed outcomes (at around 19 months), interventions produced a 50% reduction in the odds of pregnancy. But, by 31 months' follow-up, this effect had disappeared. Similarly, in a systematic review of US-based sexual abstinence and abstinence-plus (abstinence plus other advice) interventions (16 studies going back to the 1980s), the authors concluded that:

> The results of this systematic review show that some abstinence-only and abstinence-plus programs can change teens' sexual behaviors, although the effects are relatively modest and may last only short term ... Although neither abstinence-only nor abstinence-plus programs had sweeping effects on teens' sexual activity, programs that offered contraceptive education significantly influenced students' knowledge and use of contraception. (Bennett and Assefi, 2005)

No impact on behaviour at all was observed in DiCenso and colleagues' (2002) systematic review of 26 sex education trials: interventions did not delay sexual debut in young women or young men, did not improve birth control use by young women and did not reduce pregnancy rates. After appraising the findings of many studies, the authors of a large-scale systematic review of interventions aimed at promoting good sexual health among young people concluded that: 'Although sex education is an important part of young people's preparation for adulthood, the evidence is that it is not, on its own, an effective strategy for encouraging teenagers to defer parenthood' (Harden et al, 2006, p 3).

Given that there is so little evidence that sex education *actually* works in changing behaviour, it is surprising how often it is cited as the remedy to teenage pregnancy (Fletcher et al, 2008). Teitler (2002) observes that the belief in sex education is 'rarely ... countered by academic researchers' (p 141). He also notes that sex education varies among European nations, and therefore is only one of a possible number of factors affecting teenage fertility rates. Northern European nations have traditionally been proactive in provision of sex education, while Mediterranean nations 'leave much more of the sex education to youth themselves' (p 144).

One of these Mediterranean nations, Italy, has low teenage conception and fertility rates, yet a haphazard approach to sex education. Sex education is not mandatory, parents have the right to withdraw children from classes and provision is sparse (Kane and Wellings, 1999). A survey of Italian youths' knowledge about sex also showed some ignorance about sex and reproduction, with more than half of 11- to 14-year-olds stating that AIDS could be caught from toilet seats (Usher, 1999). Yet, despite lack of sex education, Italian teenagers' reproductive behaviour is similar to that of their Dutch counterparts.

Of course there are other factors to consider, not least the contexts within which sexual intercourse occurs. The authors of *Teenage Pregnancy* cited research showing that first experience of intercourse is more likely to occur within a loving relationship for Dutch youth, whereas this is less likely for British young people, with British males citing peer pressure, physical attraction and opportunity as reasons for first intercourse. Despite the disparity between the UK and Italy in rates of early pregnancy, young Italian men are similar to their British counterparts in this respect: Zani (1991) discovered similarly utilitarian reasons for first intercourse among young Italian men.

So diverse are the European nations with the lowest incidences of teenage conceptions (Italy, the Netherlands and Switzerland) that they have been referred to as an 'unlikely triumvirate of countries' in respect of teenage pregnancy (Phillips, 2000). These three countries have different approaches to sex education and provision of contraception. Only in the Netherlands is sex education mandatory and organised at national level, and contraception freely available. Sex education policy in Switzerland is decided at canton level, as is provision of contraception, and thus shows some geographic variation (Kane and Wellings, 1999).

The UK paradox

The UK's high teenage pregnancy and fertility rates may be considered paradoxical from a technical/educational perspective, from a position that regards information and technical know-how as the primary solution to teenage conception. British teenagers have access to free, effective contraception, there is widespread availability of condoms, and abortion legislation is among the most liberal in the world, with termination allowed (in theory) until 24 weeks' gestation. There may be some ambivalence about how best to instruct young people about their sexuality (West, 1999), and there may be problems with sex education. This has been criticised as being too narrow in focus, as starting too late, heavily dependent on the use of scare tactics and unevenly implemented (Sex Education Forum, 2005; Allen, 2007), but it is unlikely that this is solely responsible for the UK's relatively high teenage pregnancy rates.

This paradox was highlighted when research showed that 71% of teenage mothers in the Trent region had consulted a health professional about contraception before pregnancy and 50% had been prescribed oral contraception (Churchill et al, 2000). This finding upset ideas about inadequate access to contraception among 'vulnerable' members of the community, with the authors concluding that: 'The reluctance of teenagers to attend general practice for contraception may be less than previously supposed' (p 486). Eighty per cent (118/147) of the teenagers presenting with unplanned pregnancy in Pearson and colleagues' (1995) study claimed to have been using contraception when they conceived. More recently, in an observational cohort study that examined contraceptive use among nearly 1,000 Scottish women requesting termination of pregnancy, contraceptive usage in all women, regardless of their age, was poor, with no difference between age groups demonstrated. The authors observed that initiatives to tackle the growing number of abortions should not be confined to teenagers (Harvey and Gaudoin, 2007).

Also, high sales of emergency contraception to teenagers have not materialised in the aftermath of changes to facilitate the 'morning after'[2] pill's availability in January 2001, a change brought about expressly to reduce teenage pregnancies. The authors of a study examining the impact of these changes concluded that liberalisation did not increase use of emergency contraception or affect who used it. Nor did over-the-counter availability of emergency contraception prevent unwanted pregnancies: it simply changed where women obtained emergency contraception from (Marston et al, 2005). Girma and Paton (2006) also found that enhanced access to the 'morning after' pill for teenagers at pharmacies in England had no effect on under-18s pregnancies.

The research on teenagers' use of contraception suggests that there is not a large of group of young women in society who need enhanced access to contraception, emergency or otherwise. What are the implications of this for a technical/educational perspective on early pregnancy? From this standpoint, early pregnancy and motherhood is a consequence of ignorance and, given the right tools, can be rectified. This model would seem not to be able to fully account for teenage pregnancy. Barrett and Wellings (2000) allude to its deficiencies in their discussion of the contradiction between stated reproductive intentions and actual ones when they observe that:

> The expectation that unplanned, unintended and unwanted births would decrease as women were provided with the tools with which to plan their pregnancy was reasonable. Only with current knowledge can we see that intentions, planning and decision-making around pregnancy ... is likely to be more complicated ... (p 194)

The observation that fertility intentions are likely to be 'more complicated' than realised is an understatement; one that is not likely to be wholly appreciated from a technical/educational perspective. Comparisons with other countries underpin these kinds of explanation for teenage pregnancy, yet these are built on untenable assumptions about how other nations deal with teenage reproduction: not all societies with low teenage pregnancy rates have extensive sex education programmes, and the evidence that such programmes alter behaviour is weak.

Comparisons between the UK and countries such as Sweden and the Netherlands, which have smaller, less economically polarised populations, can seem simplistic. Jones et al (1986) make the same point about the differences between Sweden and the US (another country with high teenage pregnancy rates). The greater socioeconomic homogeneity of Sweden, and its smaller population compared with the US and the UK also facilitate social control. In such a setting, sex education programmes may be more effective. Features of the Swedish benefit/employment system might also lead to the postponement of fertility: parental leave benefit in Sweden is based on income earned just before child bearing, so there is an incentive to attain as high an income as possible before the birth of a child (Andersson, 2001).

Ultimately, technical/educational approaches are characterised by their failure to appreciate the 'social situation' that prevails in different countries. This reduces the power of cross-national comparisons, although it does not render them valueless, *and* limits understanding of the complex, nation-specific social contexts within which individual sexual and reproductive behaviour occurs.

The national context: demography and youth transitions

Comparisons between the UK and other countries usually do not incorporate a full understanding of the salient features of British society that make teenage pregnancy more 'understandable' from both an international and a national perspective. Yet, it is only by considering these features that we can begin to make sense of the British experience of teenage pregnancy.

Demographic trends and context

Teenage sexual and reproductive behaviour tends to be treated as distinct and wholly different from that of older age groups, as if there were no relationship between these populations. Examination of trends in (and other aspects of) teenage pregnancy should properly be undertaken alongside analysis of trends in other age groups, and also in the more general context of changes in the family. In some respects, the behaviours of teenagers mirror those of older age groups, though some evidence of polarisation by age group (and social class) is emerging.

The key changes in family life that are relevant to the present discussion include the decline in fertility and increase in age at first birth, the reduction in marriage and the growth of lone parenthood. There is a large literature on fertility decline in developed nations, and many reasons cited for its occurrence. In a wide-ranging review of fertility decline in OECD countries, these reasons fall into either a broad 'structural' category which includes factors such as participation in education (which causes delay in first birth among women), income, labour market conditions (which make combining work and parenthood difficult) and marital status, or a category covering 'attitudes and values', which includes greater gender equity and women's desire for independence. The authors also note that there is some evidence of a gap between women's stated child bearing intentions and the reality, suggesting that there are constraints on women's fertility decisions (d'Addio and d'Ercole, 2005).

While fertility rates have declined in the UK, these are still relatively high in the context of Western Europe (the total fertility rate was 1.84 children per woman in the UK in 2006; ONS, 2007), and high (or relatively high) fertility rates can go hand in hand with high teenage fertility rates. Bradshaw and colleagues (2005) note a significant positive correlation between the total (period) fertility rate and teenage fertility in a number of countries. This suggests that there is a relationship between fertility in older age groups and adolescent fertility (Teitler, 2002) and that social factors may be present that affect reproductive behaviour in all age groups, or a pervasive fertility 'environment' within which individuals make decisions about reproduction.

Importantly, child bearing among teenagers in the UK occurs in an environment where child bearing more generally begins at earlier ages than it does in many other European nations. This is still the case, despite an increase in age at first birth. In 2000, mean age at child bearing in the UK was 28.51 years. By 2006, this had increased to 29.17. Among 30 European countries where data are available, this puts the UK in position 19, behind Spain (30.88), the Netherlands (30.58), Sweden (30.53) and France (29.72) (Eurostat, 2006). These differentials may not seem significant but they do confirm that the British fertility environment is still oriented to child bearing at younger ages, and also that there may be a relationship between teenage child bearing and that of older women (Teitler, 2002).

In respect of the timing of child bearing, the UK is more like other Anglophone countries than many of its Western and Northern European neighbours. And where comparisons between countries are made, they might be better made between the UK and the US, Canada, Australia and New Zealand. As Chandola et al (2001) point out, there seems to be 'a statistically distinctive set of demographic attributes common to the English-speaking populations which make them stand out as a group in conventional statistical analysis when compared with the other countries of the Western world' (p 360). These authors describe youthful fertility, relatively high fertility and young age at marriage, and also 'substantial and protracted baby booms' as the features (more or less) common to these countries. Some Eastern European countries also have similar features.

The relationship between teenagers' behaviour and that of older groups is changing as age at first birth among mothers has risen, thus revealing teenage mothers to be a more distinct demographic group (Simpson, 2006). Despite a relationship between different age groups in respect of reproduction, the family formation behaviour of teenagers always represented a more extreme version of the behaviour of the general population. Rates of youthful marriage have declined more dramatically among teenagers as compared with older individuals, for example, and child bearing outside marriage is more common among teenagers than in the general population. Partnering behaviour can also appear less stable, with more cohabitation, shorter periods of partnership and a higher chance of becoming a lone parent (Hobcraft and Kiernan, 1999). If age at first birth continues to increase (and this is highly correlated with educational attainment and occupational status), teenage mothers are likely to become a more distinct population than they are at present.

Youth transitions

Family formation occurs at earlier ages in the UK as compared with other nations, and this is also true of other transitions, such as those into work or education. It is widely recognised that such transitions are more accelerated in the UK than in other Western European nations.

For Evans and Furlong (1997), the distinctiveness of British youth transitions is partly attributable to the characteristics of the work/education provision after age 16. The provision model is not strongly institutionalised, which means that 'many young people are closer to the world of work and to "adult responsibilities" at an early age' (p 36). Recently, these accelerated youth transitions have become less pronounced, yet, despite this, Britain still has one of Europe's fastest transition regimes. Roberts (1997) provides the example of Germany, where there are qualifications and training that must be completed before young people can practise many occupations. Britain, on the other hand, is 'Europe's self-acclaimed capital of deregulation' (1997, p 63). Similarly, Galland (1995) remarks on the 'distinctiveness' of the British case, where youth appear to be governed by a model of early maturation. This view was confirmed in an analysis of European Community Household Panel data (Aassve et al, 2006) on youth transitions, showing that British teenagers aged 16–19 have the highest rates of leaving home in Western and Northern Europe. Nearly 12% of British youth in this age group leave home, as compared with 7% in Scandinavian countries.

Wallace noted the existence of accelerated British youth transitions in 1987. She observed class differences in transitions, with unskilled and semi-skilled working-class individuals living independently and starting child bearing earlier than their middle-class counterparts. Wallace's study is now outdated and refers to an era when teenagers could be 'persuaded' to marry if a premarital conception occurred. Yet, even she notes the 'moral censure' that 'creeps into the accounts of those who consider the so-called "problem" of early marriage and conception' (p 155). She also observes that, even when teenage marriage was more normative, there were calls for more education for irresponsible young women who conceived and married young.

Local contexts: the experience of early motherhood

Situating teenage pregnancy in local contexts requires awareness of at least two facts: first, that teenage pregnancy varies geographically, in often quite stark ways; and second, that in some communities, early fertility may be commonplace and normative, and that this may affect how it is experienced.

The geography of teenage pregnancy was described in detail earlier and need not be repeated here, other than to say that many aspects of British life vary geographically, and teenage pregnancy is no different from other phenomena in this respect. The concentration in some British neighbourhoods of many of the features associated with social exclusion (poverty, ill health, lone parenthood, lack of employment or educational opportunities) has led to the growth of a large and insightful body of literature in this area (see, for example, Dorling et al, 2007). Despite the British government's commitment to reducing income and health inequalities in deprived neighbourhoods, and the introduction of measures to do this, the situation appears not to have improved much (Shaw et al, 2005).

Teenage pregnancy is strongly correlated with deprivation at local authority level (Bradshaw et al, 2005), but the fit between deprivation and early conception is not perfect, and other factors, such as access to local services, can affect rates of teenage pregnancy (Diamond et al, 1999). However, the little research on exploring community-specific experiences of teenage motherhood (or the differences in the experience of young motherhood *between* communities) has shown that local attitudes to early fertility (and, in some locations, resistance to abortion) may begin to explain geographic differentials in teenage pregnancy (Tabberer et al, 2000; Lee et al, 2004). Research has also shown that women living in deprived communities tend to continue with pregnancy and spurn the use of abortion, even where pregnancy-termination services are free and geographically accessible (Smith, 1993).

For working-class young women who opt for motherhood because of personal opposition to termination, possibly reinforced by locally prevailing attitudes, motherhood can be seen to often happen by default. Yet, qualitative research suggests that early motherhood can be seen as a positive choice for some young women, one that is, to some extent, even planned (Coleman and Cater, 2006). Again, this may be reinforced by local attitudes to early motherhood. In Coleman and Cater's research on 'planned' teenage pregnancy, the authors remark on the visibility of young mothers in some locations and the normalising effect this has on early pregnancy:

> With so many young mothers visible in their (the respondents') world, the local vicinity was perceived to be very accommodating and supportive of their choice. This was reported very frequently, and the vast majority of the interviewees were comfortable with their decision to become pregnant. (2006, p 26)

Young motherhood as a positive experience

In some communities, where teenage motherhood may be 'planned' and where it is normalised by the presence of other young mothers in the neighbourhood (Anderson, 1991), early motherhood is not necessarily seen as a problem and can be experienced positively. It is these kinds of observations, usually generated by qualitative data, that were conspicuously lacking in *Teenage Pregnancy*, its authors preferring instead to draw on studies using statistical methodologies. As some commentators have noted, the distinction between studies using statistical data and those using qualitative data is significant, given that the much greater use of the former reinforces negative perceptions of teenage motherhood and diverts attention away from the possibility that early fertility can have positive effects (McDermott et al, 2004; Wilson and Huntington, 2006; Duncan, 2007).

Early examples of research that explored (besides other things) the positive aspects of teenage motherhood include Phoenix (1991) and Macintyre and Cunningham-Burley (1993). In one small-scale (n=9) study (Seamark and Lings, 2004) of teenage mothers in England, respondents expressed positive attitudes to motherhood, and described how it had been the impetus to change their lives. In Clemmens' (2003) synthesis of qualitative studies of teenage motherhood one of the main themes emerging from the analysis of 18 studies was 'Motherhood as positively transforming'. This theme was present in more than half the studies and had personal dimensions (motherhood provided a sense of identity, it promoted maturity and stability among the women), and was also related to the impact of the birth on the teenage mother's family. The author, writing of one study, notes that: 'the experience of labor and delivery ... appeared to be a catalyst for the reframing of the adolescent's fragile relationship with her own mother' (p 97).

In a review and synthesis of qualitative research (McDermott et al 2004), similar themes to Clemmens' study were observed. These authors point out that, in the UK, there is a small body of qualitative research exploring teenage pregnancy and motherhood that is clustered in two main areas: the prevention of teenage pregnancy; and research on pregnant and parenting teenagers which focuses on access to services, including housing, education and health and social care services. McDermott and colleagues observe that there is little on women's own experience of motherhood, but that, where there is, it suggests that early motherhood can have positive effects. In their review they highlight, in particular, the pride that young women demonstrated in being 'good' mothers and their resilience in the face of poverty, stigma and even daily episodes of hostility from others. Given these constraints, their capacity for 'good' mothering is all the more remarkable..

Arai's (2004; 2009) analysis of data collected from women in three English locations confirmed these findings. Among the young women interviewees, birth was a positively transforming event, one which brought families together and healed breaches. Motherhood sometimes brought about a 'resolution' of long-standing problems. One of the respondents in the study, Donna, came from a fractured family, yet the birth of her son led to a transformation in family dynamics. Donna's parents rallied round after she became pregnant: 'Me mum helps out a lot. Me mum got me all this furniture. Me mum and me dad together.' Of her son, she said: 'When he were born. He brought us all together' (Arai, 2009, p 175). Another respondent, Chloe, reported a similar experience. She had previously had a strained relationship with her mother, but: 'As soon as I had [son], everything changed, it's been brilliant' (Arai, 2009, p 175). Similarly, Caroline came from a troubled family background. She did not have a good relationship with her stepfather, but the birth of her son was a catalyst for a change in family relationships:

> With my stepfather, we never used to get along until I had [son] ... he doesn't treat us like a child anymore. Me and me mam we were never actually in the same room ... until I had [son], and we're like best friends now ... She's realised that I'm old enough to have a child and I'm not a child myself anymore. (Arai, 2009, p 175)

For some young women, motherhood was a direct response to adversity. For one respondent, her father's physical abuse of her mother meant that her emotional needs could not be met within the family:

> If your home base is not structured, there's no foundation
> there, wherever you go, you gonna feel unbalanced because
> you haven't got no balance from the home ... At home ...
> you want to feel secure and comfortable. But I never did
> feel that. (Suzy, in Arai, 2009, p 174)

Suzy said she wanted to be loved, but that she 'didn't know how to
get it. The only way I would be able to receive it is through having
[daughter].' (Arai, 2009, p 174).

US research on teenage mothers' attitudes to early child bearing
(Rosengard et al, 2006) in a sample of 247 women confirmed these
British findings. Respondents mentioned advantages and disadvantages
to being a young mother. Among the former, factors such as personal
growth and purpose in life, as well as having energy to deal with children
while young, were reported. In relation to the disadvantages of young
motherhood, young women mentioned lack of preparedness, as well
as shame in relation to others' perceptions of them.

Summary

Policy and academic, as well as wider social understandings of youthful
pregnancy, are based on a decontextualised view of teenage pregnancy,
one that is divorced from reference to social, cultural, economic,
demographic and other factors. Considered without reference to these
factors, teenage pregnancy becomes a kind of free-floating container
of its own meanings, and shorthand for social pathology. This tendency
can sometimes be seen in cross-national research on teenage pregnancy.
Although this approach is useful in highlighting differences and
commonalities across nations – and will become increasingly more
relevant in a globalised world – comparative analyses can be undertaken
with little reference to the social context within which a behaviour
occurs, and often fail to recognise differences between countries which
might limit the kinds of comparisons that can be made. This not only
limits the findings generated by this approach, but also has implications
for the cross-national transferability of interventions: something that
works in one setting might not necessarily work as well in another,
for example.

Specifically, in relation to teenage pregnancy, sex education is widely
believed to lead to a reduction in conception rates, and is often cited
as the primary reason why teenage fertility rates are low in some
European countries. In fact, the evidence that sex education works
in reducing teenage pregnancy is not strong, and other factors, such

as lower income inequality and institutionalised provision for work and/or training after completion of post-compulsory education, can affect rates of teenage fertility. Also, some countries do not have very low rates of teenage pregnancy and teenage fertility rates are kept low by use of abortion.

Teenage pregnancy in the UK occurs within a demographic, socioeconomic and cultural context that is, to some extent, unique, though it may share some of these features with other countries, especially Anglophone ones (especially the US), and also some Eastern European nations. Key features of British society that impact on teenage pregnancy includes pervasive inequality, accelerated youth transitions and a history of child bearing at earlier ages compared with other Western European countries. These features of British society vary geographically and, in some neighbourhoods, especially those that are more socioeconomically deprived, teenage pregnancy is not an irrational event, an aberration or even a deviation from the norm. In some places, it is non-exceptional and can be experienced positively.

Notes

[1] http://news.bbc.co.uk/1/hi/health/2125610.stm

[2] The 'morning after pill' is a misnomer. Emergency contraception can be taken up to 72 hours after sexual intercourse (http://www.brook.org.uk/content/M2_2_1_emergency.asp).

SEVEN

Theorising teenage pregnancy as a problem

Introduction

Among scholars who question negative depictions of teenage pregnancy, there is a belief, sometimes only half articulated, that there may be other, less politically or socially palatable reasons that underlie anxiety about teenage pregnancy (Luker, 1996; Hoggart, 2003; Selman, 2003). From this perspective, anxiety about teenage pregnancy masks usually deep-seated social fears. Depending on the era and social context, these fears could revolve around young people's sexuality, welfare dependency, increased competition for scarce resources such as social housing, changes in family structure and a myriad other things (Luker, 1996). In short, teenage mothers are believed to be scapegoats for wider, sometimes unsettling, social changes, and are not the *real* problem. In this way, teenage motherhood is the site of a 'moral panic' and teenage pregnancy has been 'socially constructed' as a problem (Luker, 1996; Selman, 1998/2001; Hacking, 1999).

The idea that teenage pregnancy is a socially constructed problem is referred to quite frequently by researchers of youthful sexual and reproductive behaviour and also by young people's health advocates concerned about negative public attitudes on young people. Seeing teenage pregnancy as a socially constructed problem provides a useful starting point from which to explore (not always apparent) policy agendas and wider, negative discourses on youthful pregnancy. However, many constructionist-oriented analyses of teenage pregnancy offer only a partial analysis, and there are other limitations with this perspective. To understand how and why teenage pregnancy became a problem when it did, the analysis must be further developed. This chapter, the penultimate, most speculative and exploratory one in the book, attempts to do this by theorising teenage pregnancy as a problem. Constructionist and related ideas are considered, and the relationship between these and the policy design process is explored. The chapter is focused on two political eras: the Conservatives in power in the 1980s and 1990s, and New Labour in government from 1997 to the present.

Theorising teenage pregnancy as a problem

Social constructionism and moral panics: some considerations

The idea that teenage pregnancy has been constructed as a social problem is not a recent one (Hacking, 1999). Nearly 30 years ago, Murcott (1980) wrote a paper entitled 'The social construction of teenage pregnancy: a problem in the ideologies of children and reproduction'. A few years later, Arney and Bergen (1984) described how teenage pregnancy was 'invented' as a problem in the late 20th century. Macintyre and Cunningham-Burley (1993) questioned negative representations of teenage motherhood in a much-cited book chapter, and Luker (1996) wrote a popular text questioning policy and public concern with teenage pregnancy and relating this to social anxieties about adolescence, welfare and changes in the family. More recently, Selman (2003) described the scapegoating of teenage mothers and suggested that teenage pregnancy is the site of a moral panic, Wilson and Huntington (2006) examined the ways in which young motherhood is created as a problem in contemporary discourses and Daguerre and Nativel (2006) opened their book with a chapter on the construction of teenage pregnancy as a social problem. Scholarly examination of teenage pregnancy as a socially constructed problem is not confined to Anglophone academics: Heilborn and colleagues (2007) have described the emergence of teenage pregnancy as a problem in the Brazilian press from the 1990s on.

Teenage pregnancy can be seen to belong to a tradition whereby social issues are made into problems for a variety of reasons, and in different kinds of ways (Hacking, 1999). This tradition of problematisation particularly impacts on young people, who are often depicted as behaving in socially challenging ways or possessing troublesome attributes. Simply because of the number, scope and nature of the anxieties that teenage pregnancy encompasses or impinges on (youthful sexuality, absent fathers, welfare dependency, problem neighbourhoods are just a few), it probably qualifies as exceptional in some respects when compared with other socially constructed problems; there can be few other issues able to lay claim to touching so many raw, social nerves.

In drawing attention to the relatively long history of scholarly work on the social construction of teenage pregnancy it is not the intention here to imply a criticism of scholars who have used this theoretical framework: teenage pregnancy can be seen to be a socially constructed problem and it is accurate to call it one. However, this idea needs to be unpacked if an exploration of why teenage pregnancy became a problem when it did is to be advanced. Hacking (1999) observes that it makes sense to say teenage pregnancy is socially constructed as a problem, but that it is not particularly useful and that there are more interesting things to say about teenage pregnancy. Something similar might be said of the concept of 'moral panics' (Cohen, 1972) and, relatedly, the idea of the 'scapegoating' of individuals or groups of individuals. A case can be made for teenage pregnancy as a moral panic (or as containing features of a moral panic), and it has been argued that teenage mothers are a scapegoated group, but these are rather well-worn theories and their off-the-cuff use can prohibit a greater level of analysis: it is easy to assert that teenage pregnancy is a socially constructed problem and to point to ways in which this is done (focusing especially on the role of the media), but to take the analysis no further. It is also possible to point to the ways in which teenage pregnancy has been constructed as a problem while, at the same time, recognising that it might *be* a problem but one distorted in everyday representations and magnified out of proportion. Just because something can be seen to be socially constructed as a problem, it does not necessarily mean it does not *exist* as a problem, or cannot be problematic (Meckler and Baillie, 2003).

One of the limitations of constructionist perspectives on the problematisation of social issues is the tendency to see 'hidden meanings' and little else (Ryan, 2004). Hacking (1999), speaking of constructionist approaches to teenage pregnancy, considers Mannheim's work on 'unmasking', written in the 1950s. For Mannheim, this is a

> turn of mind that does not seek to refute, negate or call in doubt certain ideas, but rather to *disintegrate* them, and that in such a way that the whole world outlook of a social stratum becomes disintegrated at the same time. (Mannheim, 2005, p 8)

Hacking sees unmasking as preferable to social constructionism, but Ryan (2004), discussing the relationship between unmasking and simple critical thinking skills, observes that:

> Having decided that the 'surface' argument is merely a cover for something else, the unmasker proceeds to ignore the surface and focus attention on the hidden depths of the argument. It is thus fair to say that unmasking, far from constituting a form of critical thinking, is in fact hostile to it. (p 716)

For Ryan, the unmasker alleges but does not prove hidden motives, and the unmasking 'turn of mind' goes beyond reasonable caution to the assumption that all arguments are strategic: 'Paradoxically, the hypersuspicious unmasker resembles the naive child: both fail to see that arguments can be more or less manipulative, or more or less sincere and worthy of trust' (p 721). Ryan argues that unmasking is only a problem when it becomes a 'turn of mind' and proposes guidelines for 'effective unmasking'. One of these, that the person doing the unmasking recognise the 'many-sidedness' of an issue and not consider an argument 'nothing but a cloak for hidden interests' (p 726) is pertinent here, given the tendency to see hidden interests in policy on teenage pregnancy. This is often alleged without being proven, and can obscure the many interesting things that could be said about teenage pregnancy.

Given these caveats – and drawing on existing constructionist perspectives – how can teenage pregnancy be theorised as a problem? The creation of policy has a number of elements but is essentially about the interplay between the policy design process itself and time- and place-specific social conditions, norms and anxieties. It is in relation to these that we can see how (and also maybe why) teenage pregnancy emerged as a problem when it did, in the way it did.

The policy design process

How issues come to the attention of policy makers and the wider public, as well as key players such as interest groups and academics, was considered in Chapter One in the discussion of 'issue–attention' cycles. The cycle provides a useful framework for describing this process, but provides little in the way of specifics, such as an explanation of the mechanisms by which interest groups bring social issues to the attention of policy makers, or how individuals who find themselves members of a newly discovered social problem group respond to their status.

There is a relatively large body of work on how public policy is formulated and implemented (Sabatier, 1991), which is impossible to discuss in detail here; but, since this chapter is focused on constructionist perspectives, theories about the policy design process advanced by Schneider and Ingram (1993) are a useful starting point. From this perspective, the creation and implementation of policy is oriented around 'target populations'. These population groups are the recipients of either benefits or burdens, depending on social constructions (negative, positive) about them or their level of political power (weak, strong) (Figure 7.1). Policy makers pay careful attention to the level of power held by target populations and common constructions of them. Schneider and Ingram describe four target populations: 'advantaged', 'contenders', 'dependents' and 'deviants'.

Figure 7.1: Target populations and political power

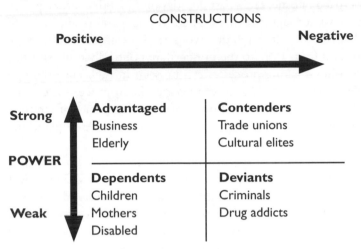

Source: Figure adapted from Schneider and Ingram (1993)

It is the last two groups that are important here. 'Dependents' have positive social constructions made about them but are politically weak, so exercise little power and are seen as in need of protection. 'Deviants', on the other hand, are negatively constructed but also have little or no power.

Using this framework, pregnant and parenting teenagers can be seen to have moved from a state of deviance to that of dependence in the period from the 1980s, under the Conservative government, to the late 1990s, when New Labour took power. The movement of young parents across categories in this way reflects the existence of wider, sometimes confusing and contradictory discourses about teenage pregnancy and teenage mothers: that they represent calamity, are conniving and are guilty of exploiting a generous welfare state; but also that they can be vulnerable young adults, or even children, in need of help and assistance. Given this, it should be noted that social constructions of target populations are not fixed; they are fluid and liable to change, although pregnant and parenting teenagers are likely to always be politically powerless, since, as Schneider and Ingram say, groups portrayed as dependents or deviants are unable to form a collective to object to the distribution of benefits and burdens, because 'they have been stigmatized and labeled by the policy process itself' (p 344).

Time- and place-specific social conditions, norms and anxieties

In a short space of time, in the last decades of the 20th century, policy perceptions of teenage pregnancy and young parents appeared to change dramatically. Although the two periods (from the 1980s to the late 1990s, and from 1997 to the present) are politically quite distinct, the same policy-making processes can be seen in each era, although they differ in substance. That is, the policy design process interacted with, and reflected, social conditions, norms and anxieties of the time and this resulted in the conceptualisation of pregnant and parenting teenagers typical of the era.

This process appears to happen on different 'levels'. For example – and at the very least – policy on teenage pregnancy can simply reflect changes in wider, sometimes volatile, social conditions and does not necessarily reflect deep-seated anxieties on the part of policy makers. There is, rather, a simple 'lack of fit' between a particular behaviour and the wider society in which it occurs. Critics of contemporary policy approaches to teenage pregnancy often argue that teenage pregnancy is only problematic because of the confluence of particular conditions and beliefs in a given social context. So, in another time and place, under different conditions, teenage pregnancy might not be considered problematic at all (Lawlor and Shaw, 2002).

In fact, and as a number of commentators have observed, in those parts of the developing world where early marriage exposes teenagers to the risk of child bearing, teenage fertility is normative and not problematic (Daguerre and Nativel, 2006). In some minority ethnic British communities, a similar view prevails (Higginbottom et al, 2008). So, from this perspective, teenage fertility does not 'fit' with the contemporary world (at least in the UK). However, there is nothing *sinister* about policy to prevent teenage pregnancy: youthful reproduction is simply out of place in contemporary society.

On another level, more deep-seated anxieties about teenage pregnancy can be hinted at in policy analyses of teenage pregnancy, especially where it is depicted (usually unwittingly) as a form of social pathology. However, teenage pregnancy is not unique in this respect, and this is true of many policy issues and is probably true in all policy-making eras. Teenage pregnancy is exceptional only in that it touches on many and various sensitive issues. It is this feature of teenage pregnancy that, through the prism of distorted media representation, gives us an exaggerated, alarmist and sensational understanding of it, and this is mostly the work of journalists and not necessarily of policy makers themselves.

The concept of the underclass

Where evidence can be seen of this deeper anxiety in relation to teenage pregnancy – whatever its provenance – this invariably revolves around the concept of the underclass. This idea has a long history. In recent times, it came to prominence in the 1980s with the prolific work of Murray (1990) and debates about the rise of the single-parent family and the decline of civil society. Although it may seem like a modern idea, there is a long-standing tradition of concern about the fertility of the working classes and other 'unfit' groups (Luker, 1996) and aspects of their life-style and behaviour. Anxieties about the underclass can be traced back for decades, appearing in different guises. Welshman (2002) maintains that the concept has been periodically reinvented over the past 120 years. He traces it from the writings of the Webbs and Beveridge at the turn of the 20th century, through to the Eugenics Society and the 'social problem group' of the interwar period. Theories of the 'culture of poverty' were influential on the 'War on Poverty' and other policy initiatives of the 1960s in the US, and its later British equivalent, the 'cycle of deprivation' advanced by Sir Keith Joseph. These developments led directly to the 1980s version of the underclass in the US and the UK and, finally, to the concept of 'social exclusion' which, in part:

> reflects a determination to overcome earlier binary oppositions between behavioural and structural analyses, but also illustrates an on-going concern with inter-generational continuities in poverty. (p 2)

The power of the underclass, in stereotypical form at least, is evocatively described by Young (2007), who examines the 'emotive triggers' that the underclass set off. These include a sense of economic injustice (since the underclass live on taxes and commit crime) and a crisis in identity (the underclass are 'them' and we are 'us' – hard-working and decent, the opposite of 'them'). Young says:

> It is surely not difficult to see how an underclass who, at least in stereotype, are perceived as having their children irresponsibly early, hanging around all day with their large

families, having public housing provided almost free, living
on the dole, staying up late drinking and taking exotic,
forbidden substances and ... committing incivilities and
predatory crimes against the honest citizen, are an easy
enemy. They set off every trigger point of fear and desire.
(p 77)

Welshman argues that contemporary policy on social exclusion is the
successor to earlier incarnations of the underclass but – making a link
between social exclusion and Thatcherite notions of the underclass
– points out that Sir Keith Joseph's phrase 'cycle of deprivation' has
been used in relation to New Labour's Sure Start initiative. Joseph
did single out teenage mothers' reproductive behaviour as especially
worrying and, harking back to older ideas, raised the spectre of eugenics
in a notorious speech he gave in 1974 in Birmingham.[1] However, in
a number of respects, and despite his high office, Joseph was not a
mainstream politician. These remarks were not well received at the
time and were not considered to represent views other than his own
(Biffen, 1994).

In summary, constructionist perspectives on teenage pregnancy are
useful but have limitations, one of which is to see hidden interests where
they may not be present and which obscure the many interesting things
that might be said about teenage pregnancy. Policy creation is about
the interaction between the policy design process itself and time- and
place-specific social conditions and norms. These can work on different
levels; sometimes, policy simply reflects a lack of fit between a behaviour
or phenomenon and the wider society. Where anxieties are hinted at,
in relation to teenage pregnancy these invariably revolve around the
idea of the underclass. Making use of constructionist-oriented target
populations theory, pregnant and parenting teenagers appeared to move
from deviance to dependence under, first, the Conservative government
of the 1980s and 1990s, and then New Labour from 1997 onwards.

How and why did this happen? And was there really such a shift in
thinking, or are there commonalities in the depiction of pregnant and
parenting adolescents that cut across the different political periods?

Moving from deviance to dependence

The Conservatives in power: the 'deviant' young mother

Conservative attitudes to teenage pregnancy, in both Margaret Thatcher's government and that of John Major, were founded on core, Tory political beliefs about the ideal relationship between the state and the family. Under both administrations, traditional Tory elements (a reverence for the family, the rolling back of the state) combined with economically liberal elements (especially an emphasis on the unfettered workings of the free market), which meant that the chief political discourses of the period were characterised by tension between a

> traditionalist agenda [that] looked ... to police the morals of the poor and saw the breakdown of social order lurking around every corner [and] on the other [hand], economic liberalism espousing privatisation, personal choice and setting the citizen free. (Isaac, 1994, p 175)

Reiterating this, Pascall (1997) observes that the governments of Thatcher and Major were built around, first, a belief in the superiority of the market as a guarantor of economic growth and individual freedom, and second, a moral authoritarianism which saw 'the patriarchal family as the bedrock of social order' (p 291). Both agendas – marketisation and the promotion of traditional family values – were promoted as means to help the state 'wither away', though in practice both involved a strengthening of central government authority. The case for the 'traditional' family structure was a significant element of Thatcherite philosophy, but it was often in contradiction with Tory economic policy. The decline of the male-breadwinner role, for example, served to undermine parents' ability to provide for their children, and mothers' movement into paid employment threatened traditional values about their place in the home. Ultimately, the demands of the free market dominated and the family agenda was pushed into second place (Isaac, 1994; Pascall, 1997).

The philosophical underpinnings of 'New Right' political think-tanks of the time reflected these beliefs. One of the most prolific was the Institute of Economic Affairs, founded in the 1950s, which published widely on the benefits of the free market as well as changes in family life. In relation to the latter, *The emerging British underclass* (Murray, 1990) and *Families without fatherhood* (Dennis and Erdos, 1992) were significant publications, with the authors of both arguing that the family was in a state of crisis because traditional family forms were being eroded by a generous welfare state. These ideas were widely reported in the press and influenced political statements, with various ministers (John Redwood in particular) arguing for the strengthening of the two-parent family. Proposing changes to homelessness legislation, the housing minister, George Young, demonstrated his preference for two-parent families and his antipathy to teenage motherhood:

> How do we explain to the young couple who want to wait for a home before they start a family that they cannot be rehoused ahead of the unmarried teenager expecting her first, probably unplanned, child? (*Guardian*, 9 November 1993)

From a Conservative perspective, teenage mothers were not the enemy; it was the young *single* mother that was problematic. The attitude of the government of the day to lone mothers was striking in its level of condemnation. So frequent were attacks on lone mothers that Roseneil and Mann (1996) described 1993 as the 'year of the lone mother'. Single mothers, especially where they were young, epitomised social and moral deviance and were considered to belong to almost the same category of citizen as criminals and drug addicts, although the crime of the single mother was to be conniving, and guilty of exploiting the largesse of the welfare state. Young, single mothers were deviant inasmuch as they upset the preferred order and, following the Target Populations theory, they were also powerless, unable to resist negative constructions about them. Rarely were they ever depicted as young women in need of assistance.

Although, at this time, much was made of single young mothers' inability to adhere to notions of the traditional family form, it was their (perceived) sexual behaviour that often excited the interest of 'family values' groups. By the late 1990s, the influence of the more conservative family groups who saw unmarried and youthful sexual activity as fundamentally wrong had diminished, but, as Hoggart (2006) observes, those working in sexual health services decades later still feel anxious about 'conservative' reactions to their activities, especially in relation to abortion provision. She notes that, though the 'extremes' of the 1980s are no longer evident, there is still an ongoing debate about these issues.

New Labour and teenage mothers as 'dependents'

Under the Tories, young (though not always 'teenage'), single mothers were deviants and depicted as morally lax, sexually feckless and too-eager recipients of welfare state generosity. The young single mother offended the 'traditional' family values so beloved of the Tories, though these values, should they conflict with other aspects of Tory philosophy such as a reverence for the free market, ceased to be so significant.

Under New Labour, policy approaches to young motherhood were reconfigured and recast using new, more acceptable language which transformed deviant pregnant and parenting teenagers into dependents. This transformation meant that teenage pregnancy could not be so easily condemned, but it also meant that the lives of young mothers could be more subject to scrutiny and intervention, often in the guise of 'help'. Teenage mothers were not to be seen as 'outcasts' as they had been under the Tories, and as befitted their deviant status. They were now dependents: vulnerable and in need of assistance, especially assistance to do the 'right thing' and make the 'right choices' (Carabine, 2007; McRobbie, 2007).

Under New Labour, young mothers were not to be shunned as pariahs, as threats to the social order, but were to be brought into the mainstream so they could participate fully in the project of modernity (McRobbie, 2007). To this end, teenage pregnancy was depicted not as a consequence of moral deficiency but as the result of a failure to exercise agency. Early child bearing did not lead to moral ruin, but to chronic disadvantage, since the young mother, burdened with children, would not be able to avail herself of all that life offers. Ultimately, the pregnant young woman was represented as 'failing' the modernisation project (McRobbie, 2007). However, once armed with appropriate knowledge and technical expertise, pregnancy can be avoided by the young woman. In Carabine's analysis (2007) of the Teenage Pregnancy Strategy, three discourses are discerned: 'risk management through knowledge acquisition' (which here is analogous to the 'technical/educational' perspective); 'shifting blame' (whereby society, not the individual, is blamed for teenage pregnancy); and 'constituting knowing active welfare citizens' (the exercise of agency and responsibility by teenagers). Carabine observes that:

> there is a danger, visible in other New Labour initiatives, that young people will be blamed not for their immorality but for their *failure to take the opportunities offered to them and*

for their failure to make the 'right' decisions. (p 971, emphasis added)

The demographic residuum

Although New Labour policy on teenage pregnancy appeared benign in seeking to divert young women at 'risk' of pregnancy by emphasising the socioeconomic pitfalls of early reproduction and endowing teenagers with the technical and knowledge skills to avoid conception, in doing so it also depicted teenage mothers as a 'demographic residuum': a group left behind in a new world order resolutely built on thoroughly middle-class values of extended education, planned careers with good prospects and, most importantly, delayed child bearing. The fact that young working-class women with little education and poor job prospects do not necessarily hold these values and, moreover, cannot aspire to them (Coleman and Cater, 2006), was an aside, and did not detract from the New Labour message on teenage pregnancy. The representation of young motherhood in these terms is not a recent idea. Making a link with historical attitudes towards the fertility of the 'unfit', Monk (2007) observes that, under New Labour, teenage pregnancy is offensive not because it is about sexuality but because of early pregnancy's apparently negative economic consequences. And, in this respect, is similar to views held in Britain at the turn of the 19th century.

Teenage mothers become a residuum because their demographic behaviour (that is, early fertility) renders them so and, by having children young, they also become a highly *visible* demographic group in its own right. In modern, advanced industrial societies, the worst thing to be is a residuum. Change happens quickly, and young people, the future's 'citizen-workers' (Lister, 2003), must, above all, be flexible, endowed with the right kind of knowledge and primed to meet the demands of the changing workplace. The young mother, welfare dependent, geographically and socially immobile, ill-educated and apparently limited in vision, embodies all the opposites of this.

Surveillance of families

McRobbie (2007) describes the vilification of young motherhood, across class and ethnic groups and observes that, since middle-class status requires the denial of early motherhood, extensive policy efforts are geared to ensuring that this norm is strictly adhered to. Young women, who are 'envisaged as an assemblage of productivity' (p 732), are punished harshly for inappropriate reproduction. So, for those who appear unable (or unwilling) to monitor their own reproductive behaviour and adhere to this norm, there is increasing surveillance and monitoring of behaviour. This surveillance, usually offered in the guise of support to vulnerables, further deepens the perception of pregnant and parenting teenagers as dependents. Increasing surveillance of parents, children and families by the state, ostensibly to promote greater child welfare and protection in the wake of the Laming Report[2] (Munro, 2004; Broadhurst et al, 2007) is also a reminder that:

> Welfare programmes are intrinsically embedded in political projects, projects that are concerned with managing societal change and that are rooted in normative perceptions of what constitutes desirable social development. Welfare policies ... are technologies of governance: they are vehicles through which visions of the 'good society' are steered. (Penna, 2005, p 144)

Increasing surveillance of youthful pregnancy and parenthood can also be linked to other developments, such as the emergence of a culture of intensive parenting (Furedi, 2008) which sees parenthood as a 'project'. The intensive parenting society regards child rearing as a highly self-conscious activity, with experts to be consulted at every stage and an ever-growing array of government targets to be met by children, and at increasingly younger ages: the new Early Years Foundation Stage[3] features 69 targets for the under-fives, for example.

The intensification of parenthood has resulted – somewhat paradoxically considering that it was meant to help parents – in a loss of confidence by parents in their own parenting abilities. This loss of confidence, and fear of scrutiny by practitioners, can mean that some parents are reluctant to use services (Canvin et al, 2007). In one survey of women's experience of post-natal depression, 44% of the sample (n=597) lied about their experience of post-natal depression, in part out of fear of how the information might be used by health and social service professionals (*The Times*, 28 November 2005).[4]

These avoidance strategies are not born out of paranoia. The growth in initiatives to promote the welfare of teenage mothers and their children, especially those embodied in Sure Start and Sure Start Plus, and the proposed creation of a database of all 11 million children in England, ContactPoint, are testament to this rise in surveillance of children and the family. In Sure Start areas, there is an increased number of child protection Section 47[5] notices (Broadhurst et al,

2007), which suggests that children living in deprived areas are more highly monitored than their counterparts in wealthier areas. This also alerts us to the fact that, while all parents are now subjected to greater scrutiny, there are class differences in how this is experienced. The most vulnerable mothers are working-class, low-income and teenage mothers, all of whom have been targeted for special 'help' by the state. The fact that all parents have been affected by greater surveillance of parenthood, though it impacts on some groups more than on others, fits with Schneider and Ingram's (1993) observation that the state often extends its 'punishments' of negatively constructed groups because there are political advantages to this. Over time, however, this will become 'oversubscribed and extended to ever-larger segments of the population' (p 343), with the result that a greater array of behaviours will be socially proscribed. Yet there is a danger that, if punishment of prohibited behaviours extends to more powerful groups, this strategy will start to break down as the number of people 'whose experiences will not permit them to buy into the messages that they are bad and undeserving people' increases (p 343). Teenage mothers, however, will be among those least likely to challenge their inclusion in negatively constructed categories. Under New Labour, as was the case under the Tories, they are powerless, politically, economically and socially.

Locating the real problem

Under the Tories and New Labour, initiatives aimed at pregnant and parenting teenagers, and which moved them from deviance to dependence, can be seen to reflect social conditions, norms and anxieties of the time as well as prevailing political philosophies. While pregnant and parenting teenagers were conceptualised differently in the two political eras, the same contradictions and difficulties of reconciling disparate areas of policy, and different policy philosophies, are evident in both. Under the Tories, young single mothers were moral outcasts. Under New Labour, teenage mothers were vulnerable and in need of help, even if that help was intended to assist them to do the 'right thing' and included sanctions and surveillance for those young women who were unable to do so. Pregnant and parenting teenagers were powerless in the face of negative representations of themselves: as deviants or dependents, they remain without power.

Ultimately – and regardless of the fervour with which they appear to hold their beliefs – elected politicians, of all political colours, are concerned with prosaic issues, like establishing and safeguarding their appeal to the electorate. And, in both eras under consideration here (rhetoric and inflammatory speeches aside), the cost to the state of the teenage mother and her children was a chief political concern. However teenage mothers are depicted, whether as moral deviants to be treated punitively or as vulnerable dependents to be helped through monitoring and surveillance, if necessary, to make the right choices, it is their cost to the taxpayer that matters.

The Tories were more transparent about their desire to save taxpayers' money than their successors. Isaac (1994) says that Tory rhetoric about the family was conducted against the backdrop of 'rising hysteria' about the cost to the public purse of welfare support. Attempts by the government to reconcile often diverse issues (personal morality, support for the traditional family, the need to work and not be dependent on welfare, plus the political imperative to reduce welfare costs) meant that Tory family policy was 'consistently inchoate' (p 188). Phoenix (1996) describes how, under the Tories, attitudes to young, single mothers and changes to the services that affected this group (the Child Support Agency, changes in housing support) may have played on the idea of feckless, underclass mothers, but were largely about saving money.

Under New Labour, the cost of teenage mothers is referred to in some policy literature, but rarely given as the *main* reason why teenage pregnancy should be reduced. Indeed, it would be difficult to reconcile the desire to save taxpayers' money with the more laudable, stated intention of reducing social exclusion among young mothers, so the focus is instead on the poor outcomes associated with early fertility. In one Department of Communities and Local Government document (DCLG, 2007), however, the authors do say that:

> There is ... a strong economic argument for investing in measures to reduce teenage pregnancy ... The cost of teenage pregnancy to the NHS ... is estimated to be £63m a year. Benefit payments to a teenage mother who does not enter employment in the three years following birth can total between £19,000 and £25,000 over three years. Broad estimates suggest that every pound spent on the Strategy saves approximately £4 to the public purse, when assessed over a 5 year period. (p 6)

In both political eras, economic, moral and social concerns supported each other well to frame teenage pregnancy as a problem, but it is the economic imperative that dominates. This 'bottom line' may be hidden behind apparently altruistic policy focused on ensuring 'well-being', as it was under New Labour, or behind the accusations of immorality and fecklessness that characterised the speeches of some prominent Tory politicians, but it is present nonetheless.

Summary

Teenage pregnancy and parenthood has been described as a socially constructed problem in the academic literature, though this remains an under-analysed area. There are problems with constructionist frameworks; they are overused, and there is a tendency to see hidden agendas where they may not be present, or to look for hidden meanings when there may be other features of a problem that require attention. Given this, how should teenage pregnancy be theorised as a problem? Under frameworks drawing on constructionist and related perspectives, teenage pregnancy can, at the least, be seen to be about a lack of fit between child bearing and social norms that emphasise a delay in fertility. At a deeper level, it can be seen to be linked to anxieties about youth, sexuality and lack of control over adolescents, and also about dangerous groups such as the underclass. The latter has a long history as a concept, and can be linked to older concerns about the fertility of 'undesirables'.

All policy is about the policy-design process itself and its relationship with prevailing social conditions, norms and anxieties. In the two political periods under consideration, teenage mothers moved from being seen as deviant, moral outcasts responsible for their own 'downfall', to being dependents, vulnerable young women in need of help to make the correct choices about their own fertility. Where they are unable to do this, the state increasingly intervenes to support them to make the right decisions. This is part of a more general move towards surveillance of reproductive and family formation behaviours. Under both governments, teenage pregnancy was cast as a problem for different reasons, but there are commonalities between the two periods. Policy makers' more prosaic concerns are with cost and, while social constructions of teenage pregnancy in the two periods may be about many things, ultimately it is the cost to the state of young single mothers that really matters.

Notes

[1] 'The balance of our population, our human stock is threatened. A recent article ... showed that a high and rising proportion of children are being born to mothers least fitted to bring children into the world and bring them up. They are born to mother[s] who were first pregnant in adolescence in social classes 4 and 5. Many of these girls are unmarried, many are deserted or divorced or soon will be. Some are of low intelligence, most of low educational attainment. They are unlikely to be able to give children the stable emotional background, the consistent combination of love and firmness which are more important than riches. They are producing problem children, the future unmarried mothers, delinquents, denizens of our borstals, sub-normal educational establishments, prisons, hostels for drifters. Yet these mothers, the under-twenties in many cases, single parents, from classes 4 and 5, are now producing a third of all births. A high proportion of these births are a tragedy for the mother, the child and for us.... If we do nothing, the nation moves towards degeneration, however much resources we pour into preventative work and the over-burdened educational system ... Yet proposals to extend birth-control facilities to these classes of people, particularly the young unmarried girls, the potential young unmarried mothers, evokes entirely understandable moral opposition. Is it not condoning immorality? I suppose it is. But which is the lesser evil, until we are able to remoralise whole groups and classes of people, undoing the harm done when already weak restraints on strong instincts are further weakened by permissiveness in television, in films, on bookstalls?'

[2] The Laming Report was published in 2003 in response to the death of Victoria Climbié. Further details can be found at: http://www.victoria-climbie-inquiry.org.uk/index.htm

[3] The Early Years Foundation Stage (EYFS) is an educational framework launched on 13 March 2007 and came into force in September 2008. It is the regulatory and quality framework for the provision of learning, development and care for children aged 5 or above. More details are available at: www.standards.dfes.gov.uk/eyfs/site/index.htm

[4] This is newspaper coverage of a programme on post-natal depression that was aired on the BBC. See: http://news.bbc.co.uk/1/hi/programmes/real_story/4476068.stm

[5] See the NSPCC's website for more details about Section 47 notices: www.nspcc.org.uk/inform/resourcesforprofessionals/ informationbriefings/childprotectionsystem_wda48949.html

Conclusion: no silver bullet. Teenage pregnancy as a problem: overview and recommendations

Introduction

This book was written to explore the representation of teenage pregnancy as a problem and the ways in which policy makers, academics and the media have responded to it. Primarily focused on the period from the late 1990s on, its starting point was New Labour's Teenage Pregnancy Strategy (TPS), introduced to the British public in 1999 via *Teenage Pregnancy* (SEU, 1999).

There are three sections to this final chapter. First, the previous chapters are briefly summarised to provide an overview of the main contents of the book and the key messages arising from it. In the second section, the TPS and its future are discussed and Downs' (1972) concept of the life cycle of social problems is revisited. In the third part of the chapter, and drawing on these earlier sections, a number of recommendations are made. These are aimed at policy makers, practitioners and researchers, as well as a more general audience.

Previous chapters: overview and key messages

The first part of the book focused on the ways in which teenage pregnancy has been created as a problem. The history of teenage pregnancy as a problem was briefly explored in Chapter One. Anxiety about teenage pregnancy dates back 30 years or so: before the 1960s, *unmarried* child bearing had been stigmatised, not the age at which child bearing commenced. From approximately the 1970s on, age became the focus of concern instead, although this change in public and policy attitudes did not coincide with peaks in teenage fertility. The latter occurred earlier in the US than in the UK, but it is significant that in both countries the perception of teenage pregnancy as a problem, and the drafting of policy to deal with it, emerged *after* peaks in teenage fertility, suggesting that teenage fertility rates alone were not responsible for the development of these new attitudes to youthful pregnancy. Instead, other social changes can be pointed to as significant in this regard, most notably, changes in marriage and the growth of cohabitation, as well as the extension of adolescence, which meant that teenagers were more likely to be economically dependent on their families compared with previous generations.

Once teenage pregnancy was perceived to be a problem, policy makers in the US, the UK and other developed countries sought to reduce it (to varying degrees). The English TPS represents a relatively advanced example of this kind of intervention. It was introduced to the British public in *Teenage Pregnancy* (SEU, 1999), an important policy document that described trends in youthful conception and drew on the large body of literature on this issue. The literature was described in Chapter Two, where the factors associated with teenage pregnancy and fertility were considered to fall (broadly) into structural, demographic and psycho-social categories. As the authors of similar reviews have found, teenage pregnancy and child bearing is concentrated among low socioeconomic status groups and among young women who have experienced low educational attainment or disengagement from the education system. In some groups, the factors associated with early pregnancy and child bearing coalesce, making these groups more likely than the general population to experience young pregnancy and parenthood. Young people who have experienced adversity in early life (especially being in the care system) have a higher risk of early pregnancy, for example. Teenage pregnancy can also be associated with extreme examples of early-life adversity, such as child physical and/or sexual abuse.

The role of the media was paramount in the emergence of teenage pregnancy as a problem in the latter half of the 20th century. Critical examination of media representations of pregnant and parenting teenagers requires some awareness not only of the processes that the journalistic product goes through before it appears on the page or screen, but also of journalistic practices of using research findings in a partial or distorted way. This – combined with stylistic devices used to write about teenage pregnancy which include use of hyperbole, of metaphors evoking chaos and despair ('floods', 'blight'), repetition of key words and phrases ('kids having kids') and use of adjectives connoting alarm ('rising', 'soaring') – creates a powerful picture of pregnant and parenting teenagers. Importantly, it is a picture that can be mixed: teenage mothers can be depicted as 'beating the odds' to become good and loving parents. But teenage pregnancy is always, and must always be, a problem and a calamity. This kind of media coverage has implications for public understanding of teenage pregnancy and attitudes to young mothers.

Media coverage of teenage pregnancy intensified in the months before the publication of *Teenage Pregnancy* in 1999. New Labour's approach to teenage pregnancy was hailed as significantly different from that of previous governments. Under the Tories, pregnant and parenting teenagers (or just 'single mothers') had been vilified, but little had been done to actually help them. Through *Teenage Pregnancy*, and the TPS described within it, New Labour made a break with past moralistic approaches (especially since they had failed to bring about a significant reduction in conception rates). *Teenage Pregnancy* reflected New Labour philosophy, especially in its focus on finding a 'third way' on youthful pregnancy and its recognition of the links between teenage pregnancy and social exclusion. The policy document also relied heavily on use of statistical data and the findings of quantitative research to present the case for teenage pregnancy being an urgent social and public health problem. The authors of *Teenage Pregnancy* sought to explain (and offer solutions to) early conceptions by reference to three kinds of explanations. Of these, what were called here 'technical/educational' approaches dominated. These are explanations which posit the acquisition of sexual health knowledge and technical 'know-how' as crucial to the reduction of teenage pregnancy. Structural determinants of teenage pregnancy were recognised as significant in *Teenage Pregnancy*, but were sidelined in favour of technical/educational ones, in part for cost reasons.

The strategy to reduce teenage conceptions in England is ongoing and a full evaluation is forthcoming. However, even though teenage conception rates have declined since the late 1990s, the 2010 target will probably be missed, and by quite a wide margin. This will likely lead to a reassessment of the TPS, which will inform its implementation in the second decade of the millennium (if the TPS is continued, in some form, beyond 2010).

In the second part of the book, the idea of teenage pregnancy as a problem was interrogated in three chapters. In Chapter Five, the depiction of teenage pregnancy as the cause of social exclusion, as limiting a young woman's life options and having adverse effects on her health and that of her children, was described. Other justifications for intervening to reduce teenage pregnancy are peripheral compared with the central association of teenage pregnancy with poor outcomes. It is this association that is central to the legitimacy of the TPS. Drawing on the research literature on the consequences of early fertility, child bearing in the teenage years is considered to cause poor outcomes in two main areas: socioeconomic status and achievements (income, labour market participation and educational attainment) and health and well-being. On the whole and once background variables are properly taken into account, teenage motherhood does not appear independently to negatively impact on life events as much as is widely believed (or as starkly related in *Teenage Pregnancy*).

While many studies do find negative outcomes of early fertility, the size of the impact differs significantly on a study-by-study basis. This may be attributable to differences in study methodology, especially in the methods used to control for selection effects. Yet, even with adequate and extensive controls, it is possible that we will never know the effect of teenage motherhood on life chances, simply because we cannot measure its true effects in isolation from other powerful, explanatory variables.

Whatever the foci of the research, whether on the socioeconomic or health impact of early fertility, no consensus has yet emerged about whether child bearing in the teenage years actually *causes* poor outcomes or not. In 1999 (and to the present day) this lack of consensus was not sufficiently reflected in the TPS which, while acknowledging the role that poverty and other factors play in creating and maintaining social exclusion, still represented the age at which child bearing commenced as an independent, significant variable (SEU, 1999). It has not been argued here that teenage pregnancy is *never* problematic. Adverse consequences for young mothers and their children (in relation to health and well-being, educational attainment, and so on) may be created, or exacerbated, by early fertility. However, as shown in Chapter Five, the effects of early fertility are probably overstated and impact on some groups (i.e. younger teenagers) more than on others.

Researchers seeking to understand the outcomes of early motherhood typically perform quite complicated analyses of statistical (often cohort) data. Sometimes, this might necessitate a cross-national comparative approach (where outcomes are examined in several countries, for example). It was argued in Chapter Six that such approaches, as well as policy and wider social understandings of teenage pregnancy, are highly decontextualised. That is, they are divorced from reference to, and understanding of, the impact of social, cultural, economic, demographic and other factors on youthful reproduction. Teenage pregnancy in the UK is, in some key respects, unlike teenage pregnancy elsewhere in the developed world: it occurs within a demographic, socioeconomic and cultural context that is relatively unique within Europe, though it may share some of these features with other countries, such as the US and some Eastern European countries.

Other countries' experience of teenage pregnancy is often cited as having the potential to offer lessons to the UK. In particular, there are frequent calls for the greater sexual openness, and earlier and more frank sex education, that is believed to be responsible for lower teenage pregnancy rates in some European countries. These calls persist despite evidence that sex education has few long term, sustainable effects on teenage pregnancy. Ultimately, the reasons for international differences in teenage fertility rates are diverse and complex, which limits the extent to which British policy on teenage pregnancy can benefit from international 'evidence'. Importantly, in a British setting, and especially as it occurs among residents of deprived communities, teenage pregnancy should not be seen as an irrational event or even as a deviation from the norm. In some places, early motherhood is non-exceptional, is chosen and can be experienced positively in that it brings benefits to mothers, their children and the wider family.

The targeting of policy at pregnant and parenting teenagers, especially those living in deprived communities, is considered within the academic literature that focuses on teenage pregnancy as a socially constructed problem. While providing a useful perspective, there are some limitations to constructionist analyses. For one, social constructionism is a well-worn theory and, paradoxically, can be a barrier to a fuller understanding of the problematisation of social phenomena.

The construction of teenage pregnancy as a problem appears to work on different 'levels'. Teenage pregnancy can, at the least, be seen to be about a lack of fit between child bearing, and social conditions and norms which promote delay in fertility. At a deeper level, it can be seen to be about youth, sexuality and lack of control, and about 'dangerous' groups, such as the underclass. The latter has a long history and was particularly important in the late 1980s and early 1990s under the Conservatives, when single young mothers were depicted as 'deviants'. Under New Labour, teenage mothers moved from being deviants to being 'dependents', as New Labour deliberately sought to reframe the problem of teenage pregnancy. Under Labour, teenage pregnancy is firmly linked to social exclusion but is also related to a new, or evolved, set of anxieties. These are about teenage pregnancy being fundamentally out of place in a new world order, where fertility is delayed for the sake of education and career formation. Seen this way, teenage parents risk being a 'demographic residuum' in this new, reconfigured world. Parenting, once taken for granted, is now a site of anxiety and – for those who might be considered deficient in their parenting, such as low income or teenage mothers – there is greater surveillance by the state under the guise of concerned welfare. Yet, in both political eras, and however teenage pregnancy was framed within the political discourses of the day, it is the cost to the state of teenage mothers that underlines policy.

An assessment of the TPS and the emergence of new 'problems'

Assessment of the TPS

Ultimately, what kind of assessment can be made of the TPS? It is probably fair to say that the TPS was always going to be limited, hampered by factors that afflict all efforts to change behaviour. There are at least four factors considered here. These are (in no order): the problems of implementing policy in real-world settings; the difficulties of reconciling the demands of competing interest groups; a lack of imagination on the part of policy makers; and cost constraints.

The latter is highly significant. The focus on social exclusion within the TPS, is an appropriate and welcome one but the full implications of this have not been realised, presumably for reasons of expense. As other commentators have observed (Fallon, 2006; Duncan, 2007), this meant that solutions for teenage pregnancy were piecemeal and focused on changing motivations at an individual level, rather than on tackling structural inequality (Levitas, 1998). Wider, macro-level initiatives to reduce socioeconomic inequalities, such as the introduction of Working Families Tax Credits,[1] have failed to make a significant impact on poverty, and inequalities are still trenchant, with evidence of rising levels of poverty across different population groups.

Policy makers have an imperfect understanding of the limitations of implementing policy in real-world settings (Arai et al, 2005) and are, quite naturally, keen to attribute changes in behaviours or other outcomes to their own initiatives. Much has been made of the reductions in teenage conceptions to date, but would these have been achieved anyway? The 2005 evaluation of the TPS used data from the period 1998–2002. Over this time, there was a 9.8% decrease in teenage pregnancy, suggesting that the TPS has been successful in its aim to reduce rates (Wellings et al, 2005). Yet, as the evaluators of the TPS admit, the Strategy did not 'get off the ground' until two years after 1998, with the start of the media campaign in October 2000. So, not only were teenage pregnancy and fertility rates relatively low (and declining) at the start of the TPS, reduction thereafter cannot be entirely attributed to the TPS without using what might be considered statistical 'sleight of hand'. And, is it likely that sizeable differences in rates between different areas are attributable solely to differences in the implementation of the TPS? Or are there other factors – maybe changes in the population or entrenched cultural values – that mean that, no matter how well the TPS is implemented, it will always have limited effectiveness?

Teenage pregnancy – a combustive mix of sex and youth, touching on issues such as welfare dependency, access to social housing, changes in marriage and the growth of lone parenthood – excites the attention of a number of interest groups, the most prolific of which are 'family values' groups and, in the opposite camp, young people's sexual health advocates. These groups appear to have diametrically opposing views on how to resolve the 'problem' of teenage pregnancy (and they do all tend to see teenage pregnancy as a problem). It is understandable that a new government would want to appear as inclusive as possible when formulating policy on something controversial like teenage pregnancy. There are, however, limits to the degree to which this can be done. It is interesting, for example, that greater use of abortion by pregnant teenagers did not feature in the TPS, presumably for fear of offending family values groups, even though some young people's health advocates have called for more information about this option to be made available to young pregnant women (Addley and Mahey, 2000). Perhaps inevitably, the TPS attempted to straddle the beliefs of these diverse groups at the cost of rendering itself 'watered down'. This is not an issue unique to teenage pregnancy: all policy is constrained by considerations of acceptability to interest groups and other key players, as well as the general public.

Policy makers' lack of imagination will be further discussed below. However, it is noted briefly that, although New Labour's approach to teenage pregnancy is widely recognised as different from that of the Tories (Selman, 1998/2001; Daguerre, 2006), some of the old ideas persisted. Under New Labour, teenage pregnancy was still seen as calamitous, linked to all manner of social ills (or emblematic of them) and the cause of poor outcomes. Although the TPS was hailed as representing a new approach to teenage pregnancy, the persistence of these old ideas (overlaid with 'new' concerns about social exclusion) demonstrates a real failure on the part of policy makers to think 'outside the box'. Relatively high teenage pregnancy rates in the UK, their concentration in poor areas and evidence of the acceptance, and possibly even encouragement, of young motherhood in some communities all point to the existence of a deep-seated, multifaceted and complex social phenomenon, and one that is unlikely to be easily dealt with by an intervention like the TPS in a decade or so.

The emergence of new problems

As we move towards the end of the new millennium's first decade, teenage pregnancy seems to have fallen off the policy radar, to some extent. Teenage pregnancy is still frequently referred to as a high-priority issue, and the TPS is still in place, although nothing comparable to *Teenage Pregnancy* has been published. After the rises in the 2007 teenage conception rates, additional funding of more than £20 million was promised to help young people access sexual health services and contraception, but no wholly new initiatives were announced (DCSF, 2009). Teenage pregnancy is mentioned as a significant problem in many policy documents, but the TPS appears to have lost some of its earlier impetus. This may be related to a growing realisation that the TPS is unlikely to meet its targets, despite evidence of some decline in teenage pregnancy rates. Media coverage is also less focused on youthful sexuality and reproduction than it once was, although when teenage pregnancy is covered in the press, this is still done in the same sensational and alarmist way.

Given this, it would be useful to return briefly to Downs' (1972) work on policy cycles, the 'issue–attention' cycle, and consider it in relation to the British experience of teenage pregnancy. The five stages through which social problems go have already been described in Chapter One. Briefly, these are: the 'pre-problem' stage, when a social condition exists but has not come to public attention; the 'alarmed discovery and euphoric enthusiasm' stage, when the public becomes aware of, and concerned about, the problem; the third stage, 'realising the cost of significant progress', when there is a growing awareness that the cost of 'solving' the problem is high; the merging of the previous stage with the fourth stage, when we see a gradual decline in the intensity of public interest in the problem; and finally, 'the post-problem stage', when an issue that has been replaced at the centre of public concern moves into a kind of limbo state, 'a twilight realm' of reduced attention or 'spasmodic recurrences of interest'.

The stubbornness of teenage pregnancy rates to come down as quickly as needed, and the growing realisation that targets are unlikely to be achieved within a decade, would suggest that teenage pregnancy is probably in the third stage of the cycle, as policy makers and the public realise the 'cost of significant progress', although the relative decline in interest in teenage pregnancy (and the academic re-evaluation of it as a problem) also suggests that it may even be at the fourth stage.

Teenage pregnancy has, to some extent, already been replaced by a new public health anxiety, obesity, especially among children and young people, which would take teenage pregnancy to the 'post-problem' stage of the cycle. In a number of ways – especially in relation to coverage by the media, the role of key players and those with vested interests and the ways in data are used – the kinds of policy and popular discourses seen over obesity mirror those that created teenage pregnancy as a problem.

Campos and colleagues (2006) provide a succinct description of contemporary concern with obesity that is focused on the US but that has relevance in a UK context. They observe that obesity has become a 'moral panic' and intense political issue, and that the role of the media has been central to this: 'between 1980 and 2004, media attention to obesity increased exponentially, from 62 articles … in 1980, to over 6500 in 2004' (p 58). An obesity 'epidemic' has emerged, with specific places designated obesity 'hotspots'. Yet, these authors maintain, proper consideration of the data on obesity – which has been used in a distorted way by those with a vested interest in creating an obesity epidemic, such as pharmaceutical companies – demonstrates not only that there is no epidemic but that the consequences of obesity are not as dire as believed (specifically, mortality rates are not elevated for those who are overweight or obese). Moreover, interventions to reduce obesity are not effective. Other commentators on obesity, while accepting many of Campos et al's claims, argue that there is a problem with obesity, but it has been overstated. Blair and LaMonte (2006) agree with Campos et al's assessment in many respects, but observe that '…the risks of overweight and obesity have often been overstated, but nonetheless believe that the upward trends in average weight and BMI do not augur well for public health' (p 71).

However, it is in relation to public and policy perceptions of the overweight, the causes of obesity and the wider implications of this that we see the most striking parallels with teenage pregnancy:

> In the US, discussions of the supposed obesity epidemic usually take place within the context of a larger discussion, which assumes that the increasing weight of the population is a sign of increasing moral laxity and that overweight and obesity are playing a significant role in driving up health care costs. This linkage is attractive for those who are ideologically committed to a focus on 'individual responsibility', rather than on structural factors … Anxieties about increasing weight resonate with those on the left of the political spectrum as well, who tend to interpret the 'obesity epidemic' as both a by-product and a symbol

> of rampant consumer overconsumption and greedy
> corporations. (Campos et al, 2006, p 58)

Marginalised groups are also likely to be blamed for their own obesity: 'talk of an "obesity epidemic" is serving to reinforce moral boundaries against minorities and the poor' (p 58). Campos and colleagues suggest that the creation of an obesity epidemic is about issues beyond the epidemiological literature and that health professionals and policy makers should reassess their role in the growth of the idea of 'body weight as a barometer of public health' (p 59). Importantly, these authors acknowledge that there has been an increase in the population's weight over a generation, but they question the representation of obesity as a 'crisis' and its intensification as a problem. There may be problems with a general increase in weight (especially among some population groups), and it may impact more negatively on some individuals than on others, but it is in the framework within which it is discussed and the language used to talk about it that we see the greatest resonance with the case of teenage pregnancy.

Campos et al also briefly mention the 'cost' to healthcare providers of the obesity epidemic. While other features of a moral panic about obesity are significant, it is the perceived cost of obesity that should be flagged up here as important, and it is in relation to cost that we also see another vivid parallel with teenage pregnancy. Teenage pregnancy may be depicted as a negative phenomenon for all the reasons outlined earlier – that it leads to poor health outcomes, causes or exacerbates poverty, etc – but it is the cost of teenage pregnancy (rarely referred to overtly in policy) that is paramount. Obese individuals, just like teenage mothers, are considered to be more expensive to the state and to the taxpayer. In the US, this cost would be borne by their health insurers, although other (non-obese) individuals insured in risk-sharing health insurance schemes may believe that they are also bearing the costs of obesity, and come to resent it.

Recommendations

Even though a new issue has entered the issue-attention cycle, teenage pregnancy is not likely to go away as a problem. This is still likely to be the case, regardless of other issues that might come to the attention of the public and policy makers (obesity is the latest; there will be others on the policy horizon). In the developed world, teenage pregnancy is likely to always be conceived of as a problem, especially since an advanced policy framework has been established to address it. If this assessment is correct, and policy interest in teenage pregnancy has declined but may well resurface at some point in the near future, should our approaches to pregnant and parenting teenagers be different? Why? And, how is this achievable?

In relation to the first and second questions, there are at least two reasons why it would be sensible to adopt new approaches to pregnant and parenting teenagers. First, teenage mothers and their children are ill-served by existing approaches which are predicated on the idea that early pregnancy is always a problem. Young mothers' and their children's well-being should be at the centre of the policy-making process and, where their choices in life are denigrated and the context in which they are made is improperly understood, their well-being will be compromised. Whatever their best intentions, those working with young mothers cannot but be influenced by prevailing attitudes toward teenage mothers that see them as indications of social pathology. A wider, social change in attitudes is warranted, as well as a change in policy-makers' and practitioners' attitudes. Once this is achieved, initiatives to help young mothers and their families are likely to meet with greater success. Second, as a society we need to turn our attention to more pressing issues. The focus on teenage pregnancy diverts attention from macro-level determinants of inequalities that need addressing if the UK is to make substantial inroads into poverty. This raises the issue of how this change in approach to pregnant and parenting adolescents can be achieved. Four ways are suggested below. These are aimed at researchers, policy makers and practitioners, as well as a more general audience.

First – and thinking more generally about how social phenomena come to be regarded as problems – *researchers and policy makers are urged to be cautious about accepting something as problematic just because it is described in a 'scientific' or 'evidence-based' way* (Cherrington and Breheny, 2005). Rates of teenage pregnancy are not increasing and the evidence that early fertility has deleterious outcomes is not conclusive. We should be mindful that, in countries where contraception and abortion are widely available, teenage pregnancy is not an 'epidemic' but rather a 'statistically insignificant deviation from the overall trend of delaying childbirth' (Lavender, 2007). As a society, we need to question more broadly our notions of what constitutes a problem (Lawlor and Shaw, 2002).

Second, the inappropriate or unwarranted problematisation of social phenomena is less likely to happen if policy makes greater use of diverse kinds of evidence. It is suggested here that *there is a need for greater methodological variety in research undertaken on teenage pregnancy and for this to be used in policy.* Qualitative research can be powerful and effective in describing the lives of young mothers in a meaningful way, and helps to provide a counterbalance to prevailing negative views of young motherhood which rely on statistical evidence (Graham and McDermott, 2005). Given that motherhood appears to have a positive effect on the lives of some women, statistical research focusing only on the negative outcomes of teenage pregnancy may be failing to measure the true impact of early motherhood. Such research might be more empirically meaningful if women's accounts of the benefits (and the hazards) of early motherhood were incorporated into the analysis. This would not mean denying the negative consequences of early motherhood – where these can be established, and which are likely to be more relevant anyway in the case of younger teenagers. Duncan (2007) has drawn attention to the importance of young mothers' accounts of parenthood, and the discrepancy between these and policy perceptions of teenage motherhood. Similarly, Macintyre and Cunningham-Burley (1993) observe that the literature on teenage pregnancy focuses excessively on the negative aspects of early motherhood and on none of its joys.

Third, and allied to the point above, *there is a need to recognise that teenage motherhood can be a positive, and even rational, event in some contexts.* If teenage mothers and their families are to be properly supported, policy makers need to acknowledge that teenage motherhood can be freely chosen, and even planned, and that it can have benefits. The TPS was created to reduce early pregnancy among 'at risk' populations, ostensibly for the benefit of young mothers and their babies. Yet, among such groups, early fertility can be normative and even desirable (Jewell et al, 2000). It may have positive, not easily discernible or measurable outcomes. Seen this way, the exhortation to delay fertility comes from a position that is middle class, and one with longer life trajectories that can accommodate extended periods of educational attainment, career development and, ultimately, partnership and family formation – in that order (Geronimus, 1997; 2003). In families and social networks where there may be a tradition of early parenthood, young mothers are likely to be accepted and well supported and, in these cases, it is not appropriate or helpful to depict teenage fertility as a problem.

The real problem, however, lies at a deeper level and it is primarily to do with the workings-out of a profound class divide. This failure to appreciate the acceptability of young parenthood in some places is linked to myopia about the lives of young people in deprived communities. Policy makers often refer to 'limited horizons' among youth, but fail to fully appreciate the implications of this, which are profound and will affect all aspects of a young person's life. These limited horizons do not necessarily reflect a lack of imagination on the part of a young person but can arise from a realistic appraisal of the opportunities and possibilities present in the immediate environment as well as one's own personal capabilities. The perspective that sees teenage parenthood as a calamity, which will change for ever (and for the worse) a young girl's life, may be true for middle-class women, who have 'opportunities stretching well beyond age 18 or 19 to become better educated, better skilled … middle class youth have every reason to believe that they will be better providers for their children if they delay parenthood' (Geronimus, 1997, p 421). The same cannot be said of working-class women, who are the most likely to become young mothers. For them, early child bearing can represent a meaningful life option.

Policy-makers' myopia in relation to youth in deprived communities is further reflected in the incredulity with which they greet the idea that young women, often in the least auspicious circumstances, might actually *want* to be mothers. Young women usually do not express these fertility intentions openly; to do so is to invite censure in an age in which it is considered strange to desire child bearing so young (see, for example, Alan Guttmacher Institute, 2002). Instead, young women hide their motivations behind stories about 'forgetting to take the pill' or assertions that 'abortion is murder', thus rendering their behaviour less open to challenge from others (Arai, 2003; Coleman and Cater, 2006).

Policy makers come from class backgrounds that celebrate the idea of 'being in control' and, when they consider the reproductive behaviour of young women in poor communities, they do so from a perspective that is wholly different to that of youth in such places (Bauder, 2002). The fatalism of young mothers reflects their class background, with its limited life options, and it also reflects a genuine desire for the maternal role. The difference between working- and middle-class women, in this respect, lies in timing; working-class women favour an earlier ideal age for family building than middle-class women (Macintyre and Cunningham-Burley, 1993; Jewell et al, 2000) and, traditionally, make the transition to motherhood earlier than their middle-class counterparts (Wallace, 1987). Extending life options for working-class women will always be a good thing, but unless unequal social structures are changed and opportunities for all are genuinely widened, interventions to prevent teenage pregnancy will be limited.

In 2006, the Trust for the Study of Adolescence published research suggesting that some teenagers consider pregnancy to be a 'career choice'. One of the authors of the study (Coleman and Cater, 2006) spoke to the media about the study findings, one of which was that some of the young women interviewed had indicated that motherhood was preferable to a 'dead-end job' and, because of this, they had chosen to become pregnant. In response, the Children's Minister, Beverley Hughes, dismissed the research saying that:

> This is an unfortunate study which, on the basis of a very small and carefully selected sample, suggests that teenage pregnancy can be a positive option for some young people. We reject that view completely. There is overwhelming evidence that, overall, teenage parenthood leads to poorer outcomes both for teenage mothers and their children. Our view is that conceiving at a very young age is not a sensible choice. (*Daily Mail*, 17 July 2006, p 25)

This response epitomises the problem well: policy makers are unable to accept that, in some contexts and among some young women, early pregnancy might be acceptable, even desirable, and be experienced positively. Instead, there is a focus on 'outcomes' and the inability of some women to make 'sensible choices'. Had this research – criticised as 'small' and not representative – come to different conclusions, that teenage mothers regretted their choices, for example, or that early motherhood had led only to despair, the minister might have endorsed its findings.

This kind of reaction demonstrates the limited understanding of policy makers when faced with the 'other' which, in the context of teenage pregnancy, is working-class young people. The middle class inhabit a world that is different from that of the young women who opt for early motherhood. Young people's life trajectories are based on their class membership, and teenage mothers can be seen to be making rational choices based on an accurate appraisal of their chances in life, but are expected to change behaviours before the structural factors that produced such behaviours are changed accordingly (Levitas, 1998).

Given that teenage pregnancy can be normative in some locations and experienced positively, what are the implications for practitioners engaged with young mothers locally? Some practitioners have reported an awareness of the tension between policy targets and their experiences 'on the ground', where policy may be difficult to implement because young motherhood is not seen as problematic and can be seen as a positive event (TPU and NRU, 2002; Arai, 2003). Young mothers working alongside practitioners in peer-education projects are also aware of the same tension, though for them it has more personal dimensions. Kidger's (2005) exploration of teenage mothers' experience of involvement in peer education highlighted the contradiction between their enjoyment at being mothers and the negative view of teenage motherhood they presented to students in the classroom. Some of the young mothers concealed their obvious love of the maternal role:

> I just say the complete truth about how Chloe throws paddies, all stuff like that, but I don't tell them the good bits as well, when she's laying in bed cuddling, and saying 'I love you'. ('Kathy', in Kidger, 2005, p 488)

Others found this harder to do ('I can't come in here and lie'). Writing of her feelings about the interviews with the young mothers, Kidger observes that there is only one acceptable story to tell about teenage pregnancy in such settings:

> it was clear during my interviews that these young women had experienced ... pleasure and fulfilment through being a mother... However, what they had to try and do was make sense of these personal stories in the public context of the sex education classroom, where there is only one morally approved story of teenage motherhood, and that is one of danger. (p 492)

Research like this was never likely to be used in *Teenage Pregnancy*, and it is absent from more contemporary policy documents. Policy makers keen to see a reduction in teenage pregnancy cannot be blamed for failing to provide evidence of how young motherhood can be beneficial and life enhancing. Instead, in keeping with the 'one story only' view of teenage pregnancy, it is depicted as problematic or even pathological. Policy makers, of course, take care not to describe early motherhood in these terms and use, instead, the language of social exclusion. Yet, they have a hard task implementing policy on teenage pregnancy in some locales because they fail to appreciate how acceptable early motherhood (and fatherhood) is in some places and how entrenched it is. The authors of a Teenage Pregnancy Unit publication offering advice to those considering undertaking 'teenage pregnancy work' in their neighbourhoods observe that teenage pregnancy can be an 'emotive' and 'difficult' issue in some areas. Local people, for example, 'may feel defensive about a campaign that seems to criticise the choices they have made over generations to become parents at an early age' (TPU and NRU, 2002, p 44).

Finally, whatever approaches to teenage pregnancy are taken in the future, *policy makers and researchers should be wary about the dangers of stigmatising young mothers, even if this is done inadvertently*. The teenage mother's 'transgression' is to have children early, when many women, for education or career reasons, are delaying child bearing. This may or may not cause, or compound, her social exclusion, but we should be wary about policy which stigmatises her behaviour. The association between teenage pregnancy and social exclusion is now made so deftly that teenage mothers are in danger of becoming a 'demographic residuum', an extreme population distinct from the rest of the population (Chandola et al, 2001) and who suffer from fertility-induced social exclusion. The government's efforts to reduce teenage pregnancy may appear benign, but there is an implicit message in government policy that teenage pregnancy and parenthood is inherently wrong. Teenage pregnancy has become so stigmatised that teenage mothers may be targeted for intervention *before* the birth of their babies:

> Tomorrow's potential troublemakers can be identified even before they are born, Tony Blair has suggested. Mr. Blair said it was possible to spot the families whose circumstances made it likely their children would grow up to be a 'menace to society'. He said *teenage mums and problem families* could be forced to take help to head off difficulties … Mr Blair told BBC News his government had made 'massive progress' in tackling social exclusion but there was a group of people with multiple problems. There had to be intervention 'pre-birth even', he said. (BBC News Online, 2006, emphasis added)

It is an understatement to observe that this is unfair on young mothers and their children, although, in some respects, unfairness is the least problem. Young mothers are aware that they are not regarded neutrally, or treated fairly, by those around them (one young mother has spoken about being perceived as 'human detritus' by those around her; Lavender, 2007). And there is evidence that the stigma associated with young motherhood is so powerful that young people believe it can lead to a kind of 'social death' (Whitehead, 2001).

New Labour has consciously not attacked young or single mothers, but it has done something possibly more insidious: it has contributed to the growing pathologisation of teenage motherhood. Attacks on teenage mothers under the Tories were more aggressive, but they were also more honest and were one of the reasons why the government fell in 1997. When the Conservative party set about remaking itself in the aftermath of its defeat, it made use of the idea of 'Compassionate Conservatism':

> Leading party figures were almost falling over themselves to say sorry for the party having appeared mean-minded and intolerant, for having alienated single mothers, gays and other non-nuclear family forms.... All were expressly welcomed into the new Tory embrace. (Mann, 2000)

Teenage pregnancy, with or without policy approval, is a relatively normal and unproblematic event for many young people and their families. Had more qualitative research been included in *Teenage Pregnancy*, this point might have been made more apparent. This 'alternative' view of early motherhood did not fit with policy at the time. But to ignore this perspective is short sighted and injurious to the well-being of young mothers and their children, further alienating a substantial proportion of the electorate from the political process and increasing their distrust of 'authority'.

Now that the TPS has been running for almost a decade, it is time to applaud its successes and reassess its aims. Given the TPS's failure to bring about a substantial reduction in teenage conception rates, it is evident that there is no silver bullet for dealing with teenage pregnancy. If the TPS continues after 2010 in one form or another, it may need to be more imaginative in its efforts to reduce teenage pregnancy. Or, maybe, this should not be an aim at all. One of the aims of the TPS is to promote opportunities for, and offer support to, young mothers, but this has always played 'second fiddle' to the first aim: a reduction in teenage conception rates. Future policy efforts may be better placed (and more effective) if they are focused primarily on promoting the well-being of young mothers (and fathers) and their children and less on the depiction of teenage pregnancy as a problem.

Notes
[1] More information on tax credits is available at: www.direct.gov.uk/en/MoneyTaxAndBenefits/TaxCreditsandChildBenefit/TaxCredits/DG_073802

References

Aassve, A., Iacovou, M. and Mencarini, L. (2006) 'Youth poverty and transition to adulthood in Europe', *Demographic Research*, vol 15, pp 21–50.

Addley, E. and Mahey, C. (2000) 'Moral minors', *Guardian*, 16 November 2000. Available online at: www.guardian.co.uk/women/story/0,3604,398287,00.html (accessed 4 November 2008).

Adler, M.W. (1997) 'Sexual health: a Health of the Nation failure', *BMJ* (Clinical research ed), vol 314, no 7096, pp 1743–7.

Alan Guttmacher Institute (2002) *Teenage pregnancy: Trends and lessons learned*, Issues in Brief, 2002 Series, No 1, New York and Washington: Alan Guttmacher Institute.

Allen, E., Bonell, C., Strange, V., Copas, A., Stephenson, J., Johnson, A.M. and Oakley, A. (2007) 'Does the UK government's teenage pregnancy strategy deal with the correct risk factors? Findings from a secondary analysis of data from a randomised trial of sex education and their implications for policy', *Journal of Epidemiology & Community Health*, vol 61, no 1, pp 20–7.

Allen, I. and Bourke Dowling, S. (1998) *Teenage mothers: Decisions and outcomes*, London, UK: Policy Studies Institute.

Allen, L. (2007) 'Doing "it" differently: relinquishing the disease and pregnancy prevention focus in sexuality education', *British Journal of Sociology of Education*, vol 28, pp 575–88.

Amu, O. and Appiah, K. (2006) 'Teenage pregnancy in the United Kingdom: are we doing enough?', *European Journal of Contraception & Reproductive Health Care*, vol 11, no 4, pp 314–18.

Anda, R.F., Felitti, V.J., Chapman, D.P., Croft, J.B., Williamson, D.F., Santelli, J., Dietz, P.M. and Marks, J.S. (2001) 'Abused boys, battered mothers, and male involvement in teen pregnancy', *Pediatrics*, vol 107, no 2, e19.

Anderson, E. (1991) 'Neighbourhood effects on teenage pregnancy', in C. Jencks and P.E. Peterson (eds), *The urban underclass*, Washington, DC: The Brookings Institution, 375–98.

Andersson, G. (2001) Fertility Developments in Norway and Sweden since the Early 1960s Working Paper 2001-020 (July). Rostock: Max Planck Institute for Demographic Research.

Arai, L. (2003) 'Low expectations, sexual attitudes and knowledge: explaining teenage pregnancy and fertility in English communities. Insights from qualitative research', *The Sociological Review*, vol 51, no 2, pp 199–217.

Arai, L. (2004) 'Teenage pregnancy and fertility in English communities: Neighbourhood, family and peer influences on behaviour', unpublished PhD thesis, London: Queen Mary, University of London.

Arai, L. (2007) 'Peer and neighbourhood influences on teenage pregnancy and fertility: qualitative findings from research in English communities', *Health & Place*, vol 13, no 1, pp 87–98.

Arai, L. (2009) 'What a difference a decade makes: rethinking teenage pregnancy as a problem', *Social Policy & Society*, vol 8, no 2, pp 171-183.

Arai, L., Roen, K., Roberts, H. and Popay, J. (2005) 'It might work in Oklahoma but will it work in Oakhampton? Context and implementation in the effectiveness literature on domestic smoke detectors', *Injury Prevention*, vol 11, no 3, pp 148–51.

Arney, W.R. and Bergen, B.J. (1984) 'Power and visibility – the invention of teenage pregnancy', *Social Science & Medicine*, vol 18, no 1, pp 11–9.

Atkinson, R. and Kintrea, K. (2001) *Neighbourhoods and social exclusion: The research and policy implications of neighbourhood effects*, discussion paper, University of Glasgow, UK: Department of Urban Studies.

Barn, R. and Mantovani, N. (2007) 'Young mothers and the care system: contextualizing risk and vulnerability', *British Journal of Social Work*, vol 37, no 2, pp 225–43.

Barrett, G. and Wellings, K. (2000) 'Understanding pregnancy intentions: a problem in evidence everywhere', *Family Planning Perspectives*, vol 32, no 4, 194.

Bauder, H. (2002) 'Neighbourhood effects and cultural exclusion', *Urban Studies*, vol 39, no 1, pp 85–93.

Baumeister, R.F., Campbell, J.D., Krueger, J.I. and Vohs, K.D. (2005) 'Exploding the self-esteem myth', *Scientific American Mind*, vol 16, no 4, pp 50–7.

Baumrind, D. (1971) 'Current patterns of parental authority', *Developmental Psychology Monograph*, part 2, vol 4, no 1, 1–103.

BBC News Online (2006) 'Blair to tackle "menace" children', *BBC News Online*, 31 August .Available online at: http://news.bbc.co.uk/1/hi/uk_politics/5301824.stm [accessed 29 October 2008].

Bell, J., Clisby, S., Craig, G., Measor, L., Petrie, S. and Stanley, N. (2004) *Living on the edge: Sexual behaviour and young parenthood in seaside and rural areas*, Hull, UK: University of Hull.

Bennett, R. (2009) 'Policy "disaster" as teen pregnancy rate rises to its highest in 10 years', *The Times*, February 27, www.timesonline.co.uk/tol/news/politics/article5811813.ece

Bennett, S.E. and Assefi, N.P. (2005) 'School-based teenage pregnancy prevention programs: a systematic review of randomized controlled trials', *Journal of Adolescent Health*, vol 36, no 1, pp 72–81.

Benzies, K., Tough, S., Tofflemire, K., Frick, C., Faber, A. and Newburn-Cook, C. (2006) 'Factors influencing women's decisions about timing of motherhood', *Journal of Obstetric Gynecologic & Neonatal Nursing*, vol 35, no 5, pp 625–33.

Berrington, A. (2003) *Change and continuity in family formation among young adults in Britain*, S3RI Applications and Policy Working Papers (A03/04), Southampton, UK: Southampton Statistical Sciences Research Institute.

Berrington, A., Diamond, I., Ingham, R. and Stephenson, J. (with Borgoni, R., Cobos Hernández, M.I. and Smith, P.W.F.) (2005) *Consequences of teenage parenthood: Pathways which minimise the long term negative impacts of teenage childbearing, final report*, Southampton, UK: University of Southampton.

Berthoud, R. (2001) 'Teenage births to ethnic minority women', *Population Trends*, vol 104 (summer), pp 12–17.

Berthoud, R. and Robson, K. (2001) *The outcomes of teenage motherhood in Europe*, Innocenti Working Paper No 86, Florence: UNICEF.

Berthoud, R. and Iacovou, M. (2002) *Diverse Europe: Mapping patterns of social change across the EU*, Essex, UK: Institute for Social and Economic Research, University of Essex.

Biffen, J. (1994) 'Keith Joseph. Power behind the throne' (obituary for Keith Joseph), *Guardian*, 12 December. Available online at: www.guardian.co.uk/politics/1994/dec/12/obituaries [accessed 27 October 2008].

Billings, J. and Macvarish, J. (2007) *Teenage parents' experiences of parenthood and views of family support services in Kent (service users report)*, Kent, UK: Centre for Health Services Studies, University of Kent.

Blair, S.N. and LaMonte, M.J. (2006) 'Commentary: Current perspectives on obesity and health: black and white, or shades of grey?' *International Journal of Epidemiology*, vol 35, no 1, pp 69–72.

Blinn-Pike, L., Berger, T., Dixon, D., Kuschel, D. and Kaplan, M. (2002) 'Is there a causal link between maltreatment and adolescent pregnancy? A literature review', *Perspectives on Sexual & Reproductive Health*, vol 34, no 2, pp 68–75.

Boden, J.M., Fergusson, D.M. and Horwood, L.J. (2008) 'Early motherhood and subsequent life outcomes', *Journal of Child Psychology & Psychiatry*, vol 49, no 2, pp 151–60.

Bonell, C. (2004) 'Why is teenage pregnancy conceptualized as a social problem? A review of quantitative research from the USA and UK', *Culture, Health & Sexuality*, vol 6, no 3, pp 255–72.

Bonell, C., Allen, E., Strange, V., Copas, A., Oakley, A., Stephenson, J. and Johnson, A. (2005) 'The effect of dislike of school on risk of teenage pregnancy: testing of hypotheses using longitudinal data from a randomised trial of sex education', *Journal of Epidemiology & Community Health*, vol 59, no 3, pp 223–30.

Bonell, C., Allen, E., Strange, V., Oakley, A., Copas, A., Johnson, A. and Stephenson, J. (2006) 'Influence of family type and parenting behaviours on teenage sexual behaviour and conceptions', *Journal of Epidemiology & Community Health*, vol 60, no 6, pp 502–6.

Bonell, C.P., Strange, V.J., Stephenson, J.M., Oakley, A.R., Copas, A.J., Forrest, S.P., Johnson, A.M. and Black, S. (2003) 'Effect of social exclusion on the risk of teenage pregnancy: development of hypotheses using baseline data from a randomised trial of sex education', *Journal of Epidemiology & Community Health*, vol 57, no 11, pp 871–6.

Boseley, S. (1999) 'Implants plan to cut teenage pregnancies', *Guardian*, 3 February. Available online at: www.guardian.co.uk/Archive/Article/0,4273,3816437,00.html [accessed 21 October 2008].

Botting, B., Rosato, M., Wood, R. (1998) 'Teenage mothers and the health of their children', *Population Trends*, 93 (Autumn) 19-28.

Bradbury, B. (2006) *The impact of young motherhood in Australia*, paper presented to the 9th Annual Labour Econometrics Workshop, Adelaide, 11–12 August, Sydney, Australia: Social Policy Research Centre University of New South Wales.

Bradshaw, J., Finch, N. and Miles, J.N.V. (2005) 'Deprivation and variations in teenage conceptions and abortions in England', *Journal of Family Planning & Reproductive Health Care*, vol 31, no 1, pp 15–19.

Bradshaw, J., Finch, N. and Soo, D. (2005) 'Can Policy Influence Fertility?', Paper for the Twelfth International Research Seminar Foundation for International Studies in Social Security 'Social Security and the Labour market in an Ageing Society', Sigtunahojden Sigtuna, Sweden, 11-13 June.

Breheny, M. and Stephens, C. (2007a) 'Individual responsibility and social constraint: the construction of adolescent motherhood in social scientific research', *Culture Health & Sexuality*, vol 9, no 4, pp 333–46.

Breheny, M. and Stephens, C. (2007b) 'Irreconcilable differences: Health professionals' constructions of adolescence and motherhood', *Social Science & Medicine*, vol 64, no 1, pp 112–24.

Brewster, K.L. (1994) 'Neighborhood context and the transition to sexual activity among young Black women', *Demography*, vol 31, no 4, pp 603–14.

Brindis, C.D. (2006) 'A public health success: understanding policy changes related to teen sexual activity and pregnancy', *Annual Review of Public Health*, vol 27, pp 277 95.

Broadhurst, K., Mason, C. and Grover, C. (2007) 'Sure Start and the "re-authorization" of Section 47 child protection practices', *Critical Social Policy*, vol 27, pp 443.

Bronfenbrenner, U. (1979) *The ecology of human development: Experiments by nature and design*, Cambridge, MA: Harvard University Press.

Brown, D. (1999) 'Cock of the North', *Guardian*, 2 September. Available online at: www.guardian.co.uk/news/1999/sep/02/derekbrown [accessed 22 October 2008].

Buhi, E.R. and Goodson, P. (2007) 'Predictors of adolescent sexual behavior and intention: a theory-guided systematic review', *The Journal of Adolescent Health: Official publication of the Society for Adolescent Medicine*, vol 40, no 1, pp 4–21.

Bullen, E., Kenway, J. and Hey, V. (2000) 'New Labour, social exclusion and educational risk management: the case of "gymslip mums"', *British Educational Research Journal*, vol 26, no 4, pp 441–56.

Bunting, L. and McAuley, C. (2004) 'Research review: Teenage pregnancy and parenthood: the role of fathers', *Child & Family Social Work*, vol 9, no 3, pp 295–303.

Burtney, E. (2000) *Teenage sexuality in Scotland: Evidence into action*, Edinburgh, Scotland: Health Education Board for Scotland.

Burton, L.M. and Jarrett, R.L. (2000) 'In the mix, yet on the margins: the place of families in urban neighborhood and child development research', *Journal of Marriage & the Family*, vol 62, no, pp 1114–35.

Buston, K., Williamson, L. and Hart, G. (2007) 'Young women under 16 years with experience of sexual intercourse: who becomes pregnant?', *Journal of Epidemiology & Community Health*, vol 61, no 3, pp 221–5.

Campos, P., Saguy, A., Ernsberger, P., Oliver, E. and Gaesser, G. (2006) 'The epidemiology of overweight and obesity: public health crisis or moral panic?' *International Journal of Epidemiology*, vol 35, no 1, pp 55–60.

Canvin, K., Jones, C., Marttila, A., Burstrom, B. and Whitehead, M. (2007) 'Can I risk using public services? Perceived consequences of seeking help and health care among households living in poverty: qualitative study', *Journal of Epidemiology & Community Health*, vol 61, no 11, pp 984–9.

Carabine, J. (2007) 'New Labour's teenage pregnancy policy – constituting knowing responsible citizens?', *Cultural Studies*, vol 21, pp 952–73.

Chandola, T., Coleman, D.A. and Hiorns, R.W. (2001) *Heterogeneous fertility patterns in the English-speaking world. Results from Australia, Canada, New Zealand and the United States*, presentation, EAPS Population Conference, Helsinki, 7–9 June.

Chase, E., Maxwell, C., Knight, A. and Aggleton, P. (2006) 'Pregnancy and parenthood among young people in and leaving care: what are the influencing factors, and what makes a difference in providing support?', *Journal of Adolescence*, vol 29, no 3, pp 437–51.

Cheesbrough, S., Ingham, R. and Massey, D. (2002) *Reducing the rate of teenage conceptions: A review of the international evidence on preventing and reducing teenage conceptions: The United States, Canada, Australia and New Zealand*, London, UK: Health Education Authority.

Chen, X.K., Wen, S.W., Fleming, N., Demissie, K., Rhoads, G.G. and Walker, M. (2007) 'Teenage pregnancy and adverse birth outcomes: a large population based retrospective cohort study', *International Journal of Epidemiology*, vol 36, no 2, pp 368–73.

Cherrington, J. and Breheny, M. (2005) 'Politicizing dominant discursive constructions about teenage pregnancy: re-locating the subject as social', *Health*, vol 9, no 1, pp 89–111.

Chesson, H.W., Leichliter, J.S., Zimet, G.D., Rosenthal, S.L., Bernstein, D.I. and Fife, K.H. (2006) 'Discount rates and risky sexual behaviors among teenagers and young adults', *Journal of Risk & Uncertainty*, vol 32, no 3, pp 217–30.

Chevalier, A. and Viitanen, T.K. (2003) 'The long-run labour market consequences of teenage motherhood in Britain', *Journal of Population Economics*, vol 16, no 2, pp 323–43.

Churchill, D., Allen, J., Pringle, M., Hippisley-Cox, J., Ebdon, D., Macpherson, M. and Bradley, S. (2000) 'Consultation patterns and provision of contraception in general practice before teenage pregnancy: case-control study', *BMJ (Clinical research ed)*, vol 321, no 7259, pp 486–9.

Clemmens, D. (2003) 'Adolescent motherhood: a metasynthesis of qualitative studies', *The American Journal of Maternal and Child Nursing*, vol 28, no 2, pp 93–9.

Cohen, S. (1972) *Folk devils and moral panics*, St Albans, UK: Paladin.

Coleman, L. and Cater, S. (2005) 'A qualitative study of the relationship between alcohol consumption and risky sex in adolescents', *Archives of Sexual Behavior*, vol 34, no 6, pp 649–61.

Coleman, L. and Cater, S. (2006) '"Planned" teenage pregnancy: perspectives of young women from disadvantaged backgrounds in England', *Journal of Youth Studies*, vol 9, no 5, pp 593–614.

Coley, R.L. and Chase-Lansdale, P.L. (1998) 'Adolescent pregnancy and parenthood: recent evidence and future directions', *American Psychologist*, vol 53, no 2, pp 152–66.

Cook, H. (2007) 'Teenage pregnancy in England: a historical perspective', in P. Baker, K. Guthrie, C. Hutchinson, R. Kane and K. Wellings (eds) *Teenage pregnancy and reproductive health*, London: RCOG Press, pp 3–16.

Coory, M. (2000) 'Trends in birth rates for teenagers in Queensland, 1988 to 1997: an analysis by economic disadvantage and geographic remoteness', *Australian & New Zealand Journal of Public Health*, vol 24, no 3, pp 316–9.

Corcoran, J. and Pillai, V.K. (2007) 'Effectiveness of secondary pregnancy prevention programs: a meta-analysis', *Research on Social Work Practice*, vol 17, no 1, pp 5–18.

Crane, J. (1991) 'The epidemic theory of ghettos and neighborhood effects on dropping out and teenage childbearing', *American Journal of Sociology*, vol 96, no 5, pp 1226–59.

Cunnington, A.J. (2001) 'What's so bad about teenage pregnancy?', *The Journal of Family Planning & Reproductive Health Care*, vol 27, no 1, pp 36–41.

Curtis, K., Sinha, S., Jayakody, A., Viner, R., Roberts, H. and the Research with East London Adolescents Community Health Survey (RELACHS) (2005) *Contraception and unsafe sex in East London teenagers: Protective and risk factors for use of contraception among black and minority ethnic young people in East London*, London: Department of Health and DfES.

d'Addio, A.C. and d'Ercole, M.M. (2005) *Trends and determinants of fertility rates. The role of policies*, OECD Social Employment and Migration Working Papers, No 27, France: OECD Publishing.

Daguerre, A. (2006) 'Teenage pregnancy and parenthood in England', in A. Daguerre and C. Nativel (eds) *When children become parents: Welfare state responses to teenage pregnancy*, Bristol: The Policy Press, pp 67–88.

Daguerre, A. and Nativel, C. (2006) 'Introduction: The construction of teenage pregnancy as a problem' in A. Daguerre and C. Nativel (eds) *When children become parents: Welfare state responses to teenage pregnancy*, Bristol: The Policy Press, pp 1-18.

Danziger, S.K. (1995) 'Family life and teenage pregnancy in the inner-city: experiences of African-American youth', *Children & Youth Services Review*, vol 17, no 1–2, pp 183–202.

Darroch, J.E., Singh, S. and Frost, J.J. (2001) 'Differences in teenage pregnancy rates among five developed countries: the roles of sexual activity and contraceptive use', *Family Planning Perspectives*, vol 33, no 6, pp 244–50.

Dawson, N., Hosie, A. (with Meadows, S., Selman, P. and Speak, S.) (2005) *The education of pregnant young women and young mothers in England*, Bristol: University of Bristol.

DCSF (Department for Children, Schools and Families) (2008) *Getting maternity services right for pregnant teenagers and young fathers*, London: DCSF, Crown Copyright.

DCSF (2009) *More cash for contraception*, press release, available at: www.dcsf.gov.uk/pns/DisplayPN.cgi?pn_id=2009_0041 [accessed: 21/04/09].

DCLG (Department for Communities and Local Government) (2007) *Common themes: Local Strategic Partnerships and teenage pregnancy*, London: DCLG.

de Jonge, A. (2001) 'Support for teenage mothers: a qualitative study into the views of women about the support they received as teenage mothers', *Journal of Advanced Nursing*, vol 36, no 1, pp 49–57.

Dennis, N. and Erdos, G. (1992) *Families without fatherhood*, London, UK: Institute of Economic Affairs Health and Welfare Unit, London.

DfES (Department for Education and Skills) (2006) *Teenage pregnancy: Accelerating the strategy to 2010*, London: DfES.

DH (Department of Health) (1998) *Health of the nation: A policy assessed (executive summary)*, London: DH.

DH and TPS (DfES) (2004) *Long-term consequences of teenage births for parents and their children*, Teenage Pregnancy Research Programme research briefing, London, UK: DH and TPS (DfES).

Dharmalingam, A. (2004) 'Reproductivity' in J.S. Siegel, D. Swanson and H.S. Shryock (eds) *The methods and materials of demography* , Emerald Group Publishing.

Diamond, I., Clements, S., Stone, N. and Ingham, R. (1999) 'Spatial variation in teenage conceptions in south and west England', *Journal of the Royal Statistical Society: Series A (Statistics in Society)*, vol 162, no 3, pp 273–89.

DiCenso, A., Guyatt, G., Willan, A. and Griffith, L. (2002) 'Interventions to reduce unintended pregnancies among adolescents: systematic review of randomised controlled trials', BMJ, vol 324, no 7351, pp 1426-30.

Dietz, R. (2002) 'The estimation of neighborhood effects in the social sciences: an interdisciplinary approach', *Social Science Research*, vol 31, no 4, pp 539–75.

Doig, A. (2001) 'Sleaze: picking up the threads or "Back to Basics" scandals?', *Parliamentary Affairs*, vol 54, no 2, pp 360–75.

Dorling, D., Rigby, J., Wheeler, B., Ballas, D., Thomas, B., Fahmy, E., Gordon, D. and Lupton, R. (2007) *Poverty, wealth and place in Britain, 1968 to 2005*, Bristol: The Policy Press.

Doskoch, P. (2007) 'Teenagers report both positive and negative consequences from sex', *Perspectives on Sexual & Reproductive Health*, vol 39, no 2, pp 120–1.

Downs, A. (1972) 'Up and down with ecology. The "issue-attention Cycle"', Available online at: www.anthonydowns.com/upanddown. htm [accessed: 16/04/09].

Drummond, R.J. and Hansford, S.G. (1990) 'Dimensions of self-concept of pregnant unwed teens', *The Journal of Psychology*, vol 125, no 1, pp 65–9.

Duncan, S. (2007) 'What's the problem with teenage parents? And what's the problem with policy?', *Critical Social Policy*, vol 27, no 3, pp 307–34.

East, P.L. (1999) 'The first teenage pregnancy in the family: does it affect mothers' parenting, attitudes to mother–adolescent communication', *Journal of Marriage and the Family*, vol 61, no 2, pp 306–19.

East, P.L., Reyes, B.T. and Horn, E.J. (2007) 'Association between adolescent pregnancy and a family history of teenage births', *Perspectives on Sexual & Reproductive Health*, vol 39, no 2, pp 108–15.

Ekstrand, M., Tyden, T., Darj, E. and Larsson, M. (2007) 'Preventing pregnancy: a girls' issue. Seventeen-year-old Swedish boys' perceptions on abortion, reproduction and use of contraception', *European Journal of Contraception & Reproductive Health Care*, vol 12, no 2, pp 111–18.

Erdmans, M.P. and Black, T. (2008) 'What they tell you to forget: from child sexual abuse to adolescent motherhood', *Qualitative Health Research*, vol 18, no 1, pp 77–89.

Eurostat (2006) Mean age of women at childbearing, accessed online at: http://epp.eurostat.ec.europa.eu/tgm/table.do?tab=table&init=1 &plugin=0&language=en&pcode=tps00017 [accessed: 21/04/09].

Evans, A. (2003) 'The outcome of teenage pregnancy: temporal and spatial trends', *People and Place*, vol 11, no 2, 39–49.

Evans, D. (2006) '"We do not use the word 'crisis' lightly ...": sexual health policy in the United Kingdom', *Policy Studies*, vol 27, no 3, pp 235–52.

Evans, K. and Furlong, A. (1997) 'Metaphors of youth transitions: niches, pathways, trajectories or navigations', in J. Bynner, L. Chisholm and A. Furlong (eds) *Youth, citizenship and social change in a European context*, Aldershot, UK: Ashgate, pp 17–41.

Evans, W.N., Oates, W.E. and Schwab, R.M. (1992) 'Measuring peer group effects: a study of teenage behavior', *Journal of Political Economy*, vol 100, no 5, pp 966–91.

Fallon, D. (2006) 'To "raise dream and ambition" – the rhetorical analysis of a teenage pregnancy strategy', *Nursing Inquiry*, vol 13, no 3, pp 186–93.

Fields, J. (2005) '"Children having children": Race, innocence, and sexuality education', *Social Problems*, vol 52, no 4, pp 549–71.

Fletcher, A., Harden, A., Brunton, G., Oakley, A. and Bonell, C. (2008) 'Interventions addressing the social determinants of teenage pregnancy', *Health Education*, vol 108, no 1, pp 29–39.

Fletcher, J.M. and Wolfe, B.L. (2008) *Education and labor market consequences of teenage childbearing: Evidence using the timing of pregnancy outcomes and community fixed effects*, NBER Working Papers, 13847, New York, US: National Bureau of Economic Research, Inc.

Francesconi, M. (2008) 'Adult outcomes for children of teenage mothers', *Scandinavian Journal of Economics*, vol 110, no 1, pp 93–117.

Furedi, F. (2008) *Paranoid parenting* (2nd edn), London: Continuum International Publishing Group Ltd.

Furstenberg, F.F., Jr (1991) 'As the pendulum swings: teenage childbearing and social concern', *Family Relations*, vol 40, no 2, pp 127–38.

Furstenberg, F.F., Jr, Cook, T.D. and Eccles, J. (2000) *Managing to make it: Urban families and adolescent success*, Chicago, US: University Of Chicago Press.

Galavotti, C. and Green, D.C. (2006) 'England's national teenage pregnancy strategy', *Lancet*, vol 368, no 9550, pp 1846–8.

Galland, O. (1995), 'Introduction: what is youth?', in A. Cavalli, and O. Galland (eds), *Youth in Europe*, London: Cassell, pp 1–6.

Garlick, R., Ineichen, B. and Hudson, F. (1993) 'The UPA score and teenage pregnancy', *Public Health*, vol 107, no 2, pp 135–9.

Garnett, L. (1992) *Leaving care and after*, London, UK: The National Children's Bureau.

Gavin, L.E., Black, M.M., Minor, S., Abel, Y., Papas, M.A. and Bentley, M.E. (2002) 'Young, disadvantaged fathers' involvement with their infants: an ecological perspective', *The Journal of Adolescent Health*, vol 31, no 3, pp 266–76.

Gelder, U. (2002) *Boys and young men: 'Half of the solution' to the issue of teenage pregnancy – a literature review*, Newcastle, UK: University of Newcastle.

Geronimus, A.T. (1997) 'Teenage childbearing and personal responsibility: an alternative view', *Political Science Quarterly*, vol 112, no 3, pp 405 30.

Geronimus, A.T. (2003) 'Damned if you do: culture, identity, privilege, and teenage childbearing in the United States', *Social Science & Medicine*, vol 57, no 5, pp 881–93.

Girma, S. and Paton, D. (2006) 'Matching estimates of the impact of over-the-counter emergency birth control on teenage pregnancy', *Health Economics*, vol 15, no 9, pp 1021–32.

Glikman, H. (2004) 'Low-income young fathers: contexts, connections, and self', *Social Work*, vol 49, no 2, pp 195–206.

Goodman, D.C., Klerman, L.V., Johnson, K.A., Chang, C.H. and Marth, N. (2007) 'Geographic access to family planning facilities and the risk of unintended and teenage pregnancy', *Maternal & Child Health Journal*, vol 11, no 2, pp 145–52.

Goodson, P., Buhi, E.R. and Dunsmore, S.C. (2006) 'Self-esteem and adolescent sexual behaviors, attitudes, and intentions: a systematic review', *Journal of Adolescent Health*, vol 38, no 3, pp 310–19.

Graham, H. and McDermott, E. (2005) 'Qualitative research and the evidence base of policy: insights from studies of teenage mothers in the UK', *Journal of Social Policy*, vol 35, no 1, pp 21–37.

Gueorguieva, R.V., Carter, R.L., Ariet, M., Roth, J., Mahan, C.S. and Resnick, M.B. (2001) 'Effect of teenage pregnancy on educational disabilities in kindergarten', *American Journal of Epidemiology*, vol 154, no 3, pp 212 20.

Gupta, N., Kiran, U. and Bhal, K. (2008) 'Teenage pregnancies: obstetric characteristics and outcome', *European Journal of Obstetrics, Gynecology & Reproductive Biology*, vol 137, no 2, pp 165–71.

Gustafsson, S. and Worku, S. (2007) *Teenage motherhood and long-run outcomes in South Africa*, TI 2007–024/3 Tinbergen Institute Discussion Paper, Amsterdam: University of Amsterdam.

Hacking, I. (1999) 'Teenage pregnancy: social construction?', in J. Wong and D. Checkland (eds), *Teen pregnancy and parenting: Social and ethical issues*, Toronto: University of Toronto Press, pp 71–80.

Hadley, A. (1998) *Getting real: Improving teenage sexual health*, London, UK: Fabian Society.

Hajnal, J. (1965) 'European marriage pattern in historical perspective', in D.V. Glass and D.E.C. Eversley (eds) *Population in history*, London: Arnold, pp 101–43.

Hamilton-Wieler, S. (1988) 'The fallacy of decontextualization', *Viewpoints*, vol 120, pp 2–18.

Harden, A., Brunton, G., Fletcher, A., Oakley, A., Burchett, H. and Backhans, M. (2006) *Young people, pregnancy and social exclusion: A systematic synthesis of research evidence to identify effective, appropriate and promising approaches for prevention and support*, London: EPPI-Centre, Social Science Research Unit, Institute of Education, University of London.

Harvey, N. and Gaudoin, M. (2007) 'Teenagers requesting pregnancy termination are no less responsible about contraceptive use at the time of conception than older women', *BJOG An International Journal of Obstetrics and Gynaecology*, vol 114, no 2, pp 226–9.

Heilborn, M.L., Brandao, E.R. and Cabral, C.D. (2007) 'Teenage pregnancy and moral panic in Brazil', *Culture Health & Sexuality*, vol 9, no 4, pp 403–14.

Henry, J. (2005) 'Teenage mothers to be given make-overs to "raise their self-esteem" … all at taxpayers' expense, naturally', *Daily Telegraph*, 5 June. Available online at: www.telegraph.co.uk/global/main.jhtml?xml=/global/2005/06/05/nteen05.xml [accessed 23 October 2008].

Higginbottom, G.M.A., Mathers, N., Marsh, P., Kirkham, M., Owen, J.M. and Serrant-Green, L. (2006) 'Young people of minority ethnic origin in England and early parenthood: views from young parents and service providers', *Social Science & Medicine*, vol 63, no 4, pp 858–70.

Higginbottom, G.M.A., Serrant-Green, L., Mathers, N., Marsh, P., Kirkham, M. and Owen, J. (2008) '"I didn't do it cause I wanted a baby": sexual decision making, roles and choices in relation to early parenthood amongst black and minority ethnic young parents in England', *Diversity in Health & Social Care*, vol 5, no 2, pp 89–99.

Hilgartner, S. and Bosk, C.L. (1988) 'The rise and fall of social problems: a public arenas model', *The American Journal of Sociology*, vol 94, no 1, pp 53–78.

Hobcraft, J. and Kiernan, K. (1999) *Childhood poverty, early motherhood and adult social exclusion*, CASE Paper 28, London: Centre for Analysis of Social Exclusion, London School of Economics.

Hoffman, S. (1998) 'Teenage childbearing is not so bad after all … or is it? A review of the new literature', *Family Planning Perspectives*, vol 30, no 5, pp 236–9.

Hoggart, L. (2003) 'Teenage pregnancy: the government's dilemma,' *Capital & Class*, vol 79, pp 145–65.

Hoggart, L. (2006) 'Risk: young women and sexual decision-making', *Forum: Qualitative Social Research*, vol 7, no 1. Available online at: www.qualitative-research.net/index.php/fqs/article/view/57/118 [accessed 23 October 2008].

Holmlund, H. (2005) 'Estimating long-term consequences of teenage childbearing: an examination of the siblings approach', *Journal of Human Resources*, vol 40, no 3, pp 716–43.

Hosie, A.C.S. (2007) '"I hated everything about school": An examination of the relationship between dislike of school, teenage pregnancy and educational disengagement', *Social Policy & Society*, vol 6, no 3, pp 333–47.

Hotz, J., McElroy, S.W. and Sanders, S.G. (2005) 'Teenage childbearing and its life cycle consequences: exploiting a natural experiment', *The Journal of Human Resources*, vol 40, no 3, pp 683–715.

Imamura, M., Tucker, J., Hannaford, P., da Silva, M.O., Astin, M., Wyness, L., Bloemenkamp, K.W.M., Jahn, A., Karro, H. and Olsen, J. (2007) 'Factors associated with teenage pregnancy in the European Union countries: a systematic review', *The European Journal of Public Health*, vol 17, no 6, pp 630–6.

Isaac, J. (1994) 'The politics of morality in the UK', *Parliamentary Affairs*, vol 47, no 2, pp 175–89.

Jewell, D., Tacchi, J. and Donovan, J. (2000) 'Teenage pregnancy: whose problem is it?', *Family Practice*, vol 17, no 6, pp 522–8.

Jolly, M., Sebire, N., Harris, J., Robinson, S. and Regan, L. (2000) 'Obstetric risks of pregnancy in women less than 18 years old', *Obstetrics & Gynecology*, vol 96, no 6, pp 962–6.

Jones, E.F., Darroch Forrest, J., Goldman, N., Henshaw, S., Lincoln, R., Rosoff, J.I., Westoff, C.F. and Wulf, D. (1986) *Teenage pregnancy in industrialized countries*, Alan Guttmacher Institute, New Haven, CT: Yale University Press.

Kane, R. and Wellings, K. (1999) *Reducing the rate of teenage conceptions. An international review of the evidence: data from Europe*, London, UK: Health Education Authority.

Kaplan, G., Goodman, A. and Walker, I. (2004) *Understanding the effects of early motherhood in Britain: The effects on mothers*, Warwick Economic Research Papers, No 76, Warwick, UK: University of Warwick.

Kelly, D.M. (1996) 'Stigma stories: four discourses about teen mothers, welfare and poverty', *Youth & Society*, vol 27, no 4, pp 421–49.

Kidger, J. (2005) 'Stories of redemption? Teenage mothers as the new sex educators', *Sexualities*, vol 8, no 4, pp 481–96.

Kiernan, K.E. (1997) 'Becoming a young parent: a longitudinal study of associated factors', *British Journal of Sociology*, vol 48, no 3, pp 406–28.

Kirkman, M., Harrison, L., Hillier, L. and Pyett, P. (2001) '"I know I'm doing a good job": canonical and autobiographical narratives of teenage mothers', *Culture, Health & Sexuality*, vol 3, no 3, pp 279–94.

Kives, S. and Jamieson, M.A. (2001) 'Desire for pregnancy among adolescents in an antenatal clinic', *Journal of Pediatric & Adolescent Gynecology*, vol 14, no 3, p 150.

Klepinger, D.H., Lundberg, S. and Plotnick, R. (1999) 'How does adolescent fertility affect the human capital and wages of young women?', *Journal of Human Resources*, vol 34, no3, pp 421–48.

Klerman, L.V. (2006) 'Risk of poor pregnancy outcomes: is it higher among multiparous teenage mothers?', *Journal of Adolescent Health*, vol 38, no 6, pp 761–4.

Knudsen, L.B. and Valle, A.-K. (2006) 'Teenage reproductive behaviour in Denmark and Norway: lessons from the Nordic welfare state', in A. Daguerre and C. Nativel (eds) *When children become parents: Welfare state responses to teenage pregnancy*, Bristol: The Policy Press, pp 161–81.

Lavender, B. (2007) 'Young, gifted and pregnant', *Guardian*, March 31. Available online at: www.guardian.co.uk/lifeandstyle/2007/mar/31/familyandrelationships.family [accessed 7 November 2008].

Lawlor, D.A. and Shaw, M. (2002) 'Too much too young? Teenage pregnancy is not a public health problem', *International Journal of Epidemiology*, vol 31, no 3, pp 552–3.

Lawlor, D.A. and Shaw, M. (2004) 'Teenage pregnancy rates: high compared with where and when?, *Journal of the Royal Society of Medicine*, vol 97, no 3, pp 121–3.

Lee, E., Clements, S., Ingham, R. and Stone, N. (2004) *A matter of choice? Explaining national variation in teenage abortion and motherhood*, York, UK: Joseph Rowntree Foundation.

Leggett, W. (2007) 'Third Way (Giddens)', in G. Ritzer (ed) *Blackwell Encyclopedia of Sociology*, Blackwell Reference Online, Blackwell Publishing.

Levitas, R. (1998) *The inclusive society? New Labour and social exclusion*, Basingstoke, UK: Macmillan.

Lindberg, L.D., Sonenstein, F.L., Ku, L. and Martinez, G. (1997) 'Age differences between minors who give birth and their adult partners', *Family Planning Perspectives*, vol 29, no 2, pp 61–6.

Linne, O. and Jones, M. (2000) 'The coverage of lone-parents in British newspapers: a construction based on moral panic?' *Nordicom Review*, vol 21, no 1, pp 59–70.

Lister, R. (2003) 'Investing in the citizen-workers of the future: transformations in citizenship and the state under New Labour', *Social Policy and Administration*, vol 37, no 5, pp 427–43.

London Borough of Lambeth (2001) *Lambeth teenage pregnancy and parenthood strategy incorporating 2001–2004 action plan*, London: London Borough of Lambeth.

López Turley, R.N. (2003) 'Are children of young mothers disadvantaged because of their mother's age or family background?', *Child Development*, vol 74, no 2, pp 465–74.

Luker, K. (1996) *Dubious conceptions: The politics of teenage pregnancy*, Cambridge, MA: Harvard University Press.

Manlove, J., Terry-Humen, E. and Ikramullah, E. (2006) 'Young teenagers and older sexual partners: correlates and consequences for males and females', *Perspectives on Sexual & Reproductive Health*, vol 38, no 4, pp 197–207.

Mann, N. (2000) 'Reasons to be cheerful', BBC Online News, 17 April. Available online at: http://news.bbc.co.uk/1/hi/uk_politics/716402.stm [accessed 7 November 2008].

Mannheim, K. (2005) 'The problem of a sociology of knowledge', in N. Stehr and R. Grundmann (eds) *Knowledge: Critical concepts*, London: Taylor and Francis.

Marston, C., Meltzer, H. and Majeed, A. (2005) 'Impact on contraceptive practice of making emergency hormonal contraception available over the counter in Great Britain: repeated cross sectional surveys', *BMJ*, vol 331, no 7511, pp 271–3.

Maxwell, C. and Chase, E. (2008) 'Peer pressure – beyond rhetoric to reality', *Sex Education*, vol 8, no 3, pp 303–14.

Mayor, S. (1998) 'Health of the Nation deemed a failure', *BMJ*, vol 317, no 7165, p 1034.

McCulloch, A. (2001) 'Teenage childbearing in Great Britain and the spatial concentration of poverty households', *Journal of Epidemiology & Community Health*, vol 55, no 1, pp 16–23.

McDermott, E., Graham, H. and Hamilton, V. (2004) *Experience of being a teenage mother in the UK: A report of a systematic review of qualitative studies*, The Centre for Evidence-based Public Health Policy, the Social and Public Health Services Unit, Glasgow: University of Glasgow.

Macintyre, S. and Cunningham-Burley, S. (1993) 'Teenage pregnancy as a social problem: a perspective from the United Kingdom', in A. Lawson, and D.L. Rhode (eds) *The politics of pregnancy: Adolescent sexuality and public policy*, New Haven and London: Yale University Press, pp 59-73.

Macleod, C. (2003) 'Teenage pregnancy and the construction of adolescence: scientific literature in South Africa', *Childhood*, vol 10, no 4, pp 419–37.

McRobbie, A. (2007) 'Top girls? Young women and the post-feminist sexual contract', *Cultural Studies*, vol 21, no 4–5, pp 718–37.

Meade, C.S., Kershaw, T.S. and Ickovics, J.R. (2008) 'The intergenerational cycle of teenage motherhood: an ecological approach', *Health Psychology*, vol 27, no 4, pp 419–29.

Meckler, M. and Baillie, J. (2003) 'The truth about social construction in administrative science', *Journal of Management Inquiry*, vol 12, no 3, pp 273–84.

Melhuish, E. and Phoenix, A. (1987) 'Motherhood under twenty: prevailing ideologies and research', *Children & Society*, vol 1, no 4, pp 288–98.

Monk, D. (2007) 'Teenage pregnancies and sex education: constructing the girl/woman subject', in C. Stychin and V. Munro (eds) *Sexuality and the law: Feminist engagements*, Abingdon, Oxford: Glasshouse/Routledge Press, pp 201–21.

Morehead, A. and Soriano, G. (2005) 'Teenage mothers: constructing family', *Family Matters*, vol 72, summer, pp 64–71.

Munro, E. (2004) 'State regulation of parenting', *Political Quarterly*, vol 75, no 2, pp 180–8.

Murcott, A. (1980) 'The social construction of teenage pregnancy: a problem in the ideologies of childhood and reproduction', *Sociology of Health & Illness*, vol 2, no 1, pp 1–23.

Murray, C. (and Health and Welfare Unit, Institute of Economic Affairs) (1990) *The emerging British underclass*, London, UK: IEA Health and Welfare Unit.

National Council for One Parent Families (2000) *A secure start for young families: the housing and support needs of young lone mothers. Summary of key findings*, London: National Council for One Parent Families.

Nativel, C. and Daguerre, A. (2006) 'Conclusion: welfare states and the politics of teenage pregnancy: lessons from cross-national comparisons', in A. Daguerre and C. Nativel (eds) *When children become parents: Welfare state responses to teenage pregnancy*, Bristol, The Policy Press, pp 225-40.

Nebot, M., Borrell, C. and Villalbi, J.R. (1997) 'Adolescent motherhood and socioeconomic factors. An ecologic approach', *The European Journal of Public Health*, vol 7, no 2, pp 144–8.

Newman, J. (2001) *Modernising governance: New Labour, policy and society*, London, UK: Sage.

NHS CRD (NHS Centre for Reviews and Dissemination) (1997) *Effective health care: Preventing and reducing the adverse effects of unintended teenage pregnancies*, vol 3, no 1, University of York, UK: NHS Centre for Reviews and Dissemination.

NRU (Neighbourhood Renewal Unit) (2002) *Teenage pregnancy (overview)*, London: Neighbourhood Renewal Unit (Renewal.Net).

Oakley, A., Fullerton, D., Holland, J., Arnold, S., France-Dawson, M., Kelley, P. and McGrellis, S. (1995) 'Sexual health interventions for young people: a methodological review', *BMJ*, vol 310, pp 158–62.

ONS (Office for National Statistics) (2005) ONS's *Conception Statistics* chs1 and 4.

ONS (2006) *Population trends 126*, London: The Stationery Office.

ONS (2007) *Population trends 130 – births in England and Wales 2006*, London: The Stationery Office.

Owen, J., Higginbottom, G.M.A., Kirkham, M., Mathers, N. and Marsh, P. (2008) 'Ethnicity, policy and teenage parenthood in England: findings from a qualitative study', *Social Policy and Society*, vol 7, pp 293–305.

Pallitto, C.C. and Murillo, V. (2008) 'Childhood abuse as a risk factor for adolescent pregnancy in El Salvador', *Journal of Adolescent Health*, vol 42, no 6, pp 580–6.

Pascall, G. (1997) 'Women and the family in the British welfare state: the Thatcher/Major legacy', *Social Policy & Administration*, vol 31, no 3, pp 290–305.

Pearson, V.A.H., Owen, M.R., Phillips, D.R., Pereira Gray, D.J. and Marshall, M.N. (1995) 'Pregnant teenagers' knowledge and use of emergency contraception', *BMJ*, vol 310, no 6995, p 1644.

Penna, S. (2005) 'The Children Act 2004: Child protection and social surveillance', *Journal of Social Welfare & Family Law*, vol 27, no 2, pp 143–57.

Petersen, J., Atkinson, P., Petrie, S., Gibin, M., Ashby, D. and Longley, P. (2008) 'Teenage pregnancy – new tools to support local health campaigns', *Health & Place*, vol 15, no 1, pp 300–7.

Phillips, A. (2000) 'Let's talk about sex', *Guardian*, 6 March. Available online at: www.guardian.co.uk/women/story/0,3604,233068,00. html [accessed 7 November 2008].

Phoenix, A. (1991) *Young mothers?* Cambridge, UK: Polity Press.

Phoenix, A. (1996) 'Social constructions of lone mothers. A case of competing discourses', in E.B. Silva (ed) *Good enough mothering? Feminist perspectives on lone motherhood*, London: Routledge, pp 175–90.

Pijpers, R. (2006) '"Help! The Poles are coming": narrating a contemporary moral panic', *Geografiska Annaler: Series B, Human Geography*, vol 88, no 1, pp 91–103.

PM, Australian Broadcasting Corporation (2003) 'Teenage pregnancies more prevalent in rural areas', broadcast on 7/7/03. Available online at: www.abc.net.au/pm/content/2003/s896898.htm [accessed 1 October 2008].

Public Health Division, New South Wales (2000) *The health of the people of New South Wales: Report of the Chief Health Officer*, Sydney, Australia: New South Wales Health Department.

Quinlivan, J.A. and Condon, J. (2005) 'Anxiety and depression in fathers in teenage pregnancy', *Australian & New Zealand Journal of Psychiatry*, vol 39, no 10, pp 915–20.

RBS (Royal Bank of Scotland) (2003) 'Myths about lone parents still exist, survey reveals', press release. Available online at: www.rbs.com/media03.asp?id=MEDIA_CENTRE/PRESS_RELEASES/2003/AUGUST/26_ONE_PARENT_FAMILIES [accessed 7 November 2008].

Reeves, J. (2006) 'Recklessness, rescue and responsibility: young men tell their stories of the transition to fatherhood', *Practice*, vol 18, no 2, pp 79–90.

Reeves, J. (2007) '"Tell me your story": applied ethics in narrative research with young fathers', *Children's Geographies*, vol 5, no 3, pp 253–65.

Richan, W.C. (1987) *Beyond altruism: Social welfare policy in American society*, Philadelphia, USA: Haworth Press Inc.

Richmond and Twickenham Primary Care Trust (2002) *Public health profile*, Richmond and Twickenham, London: NHS.

Roberts, H., Arai, L., Roen, K. and Popay, J. (2006) 'What evidence do we have on implementation?', in A. Killoran, C. Swann and M.P. Kelly (eds) *Public health evidence: tackling health inequalities.* Oxford, UK: Oxford University Press, pp 299–308.

Roberts, K. (1997) 'Structure and agency: the new youth research agenda', in J. Bynner, L. Chisholm and A. Furlong (eds) *Youth, citizenship and social change in a European context*, Aldershot, UK: Ashgate Publishing Ltd, pp 56–65.

Roberts, R., O'Connor, T., Dunn, J., Golding, J. and ALSPAC Study Team (2004) 'The effects of child sexual abuse in later family life; mental health, parenting and adjustment of offspring', *Child Abuse & Neglect*, vol 28, no 5, pp 525–45.

Rolfe, A. (2008) '"You've got to grow up when you've got a kid": marginalized young women's accounts of motherhood', *Journal of Community & Applied Social Psychology*, vol 18, no 4, pp 299–314.

Romans, S.E., Martin, J.L. and Morris, E.M. (1997) 'Risk factors for adolescent pregnancy: how important is child sexual abuse?', *New Zealand Medical Journal*, vol 110, no 1037, pp 30–3.

Rosato, M. (1999) *Teenage fertility in England and Wales: Trends in socioeconomic circumstances between the 1971 and the 1981 censuses*, Longitudinal Study Working Paper 78, London: Institute of Education, University of London, Centre for Longitudinal Studies.

Roseneil, S. and Mann, K. (1996) 'Unpalatable choices and inadequate families. Lone mothers and the underclass debate', in E.B. Silva (ed) *Good enough mothering? Feminist perspectives on lone motherhood*, London: Routledge, pp 191–210.

Rosengard, C., Pollack, L., Weitzen, S., Meers, A. and Phipps, M.G. (2006) 'Concepts of the advantages and disadvantages of teenage childbearing among pregnant adolescents: A qualitative analysis', *Pediatrics*, vol 118, no 2, pp 503–10.

Ryan, P. (2004) 'The policy sciences and the unmasking turn of mind 1', *Review of Policy Research*, vol 21, no 5, pp 715–28.

Ryan, S., Franzetta, K. and Manlove, J. (2005) *Hispanic teen pregnancy and birth rates: Looking behind the numbers*, Washington, DC: Child Trends Inc.

Sabatier, J. (1991) 'Toward better theories of the policy process', *Political Science & Politics*, vol 24, no 2, pp 147–56.

Santow, G. and Bracher, M. (1999) 'Explaining trends in teenage childbearing in Sweden', *Studies in Family Planning*, vol 30, no 3, pp 169–82.

Schneider, A.L. and Ingram, H. (1993) 'Social construction of target populations: implications for politics and policy', *The American Political Science Review*, vol 87, no 2, pp 334–47.

SCIE (Social Care Institute of Excellence) (2004/5) *Preventing teenage pregnancy in looked after children*, SCIE research briefing 9, London: Social Care Institute of Excellence.

Seamark, C. (1999) 'Sexual health of teenagers. Time to put it in perspective [letter]', *BMJ*, vol 319, no 7221, p 1368.

Seamark, C.J. and Lings, P. (2004) 'Positive experiences of teenage motherhood: a qualitative study', *British Journal of General Practice*, vol 54, no 508, pp 813–8.

Selman, P. (1998/2001) 'Teenage pregnancy, poverty and the welfare debate in Europe and the United States', Paper presented at the seminar *Poverty, fertility and family planning*, Mexico City, Mexico, 2–4 June 1998.

Selman, P. (2003) 'Scapegoating and moral panics: Teenage pregnancy in Britain and the United States', in S. Cunningham-Burley and L. Jamieson (eds) *Families and the state: Changing relationships*, Basingstoke: Palgrave Macmillan, pp 159–86.

Senn, T.E., Carey, M.P. and Vanable, P.A. (2008) 'Childhood and adolescent sexual abuse and subsequent sexual risk behavior: evidence from controlled studies, methodological critique, and suggestions for research', *Clinical Psychology Review*, vol 28, no 5, pp 711–35.

SEU (Social Exclusion Unit) (1999) *Teenage pregnancy*, London: The Stationery Office.

SEU (2004) *Breaking the cycle: Taking stock of progress and priorities for the future.* A report by the Social Exclusion Unit, London: Office of the Deputy Prime Minister.

Sex Education Forum (2005) *Sex and relationships education framework*, London: Sex Education Forum.

Shaw, M. and Lawlor, D. (2007) 'Why we measure teenage pregnancy but do not count teenage mothers?' *Critical Public Health*, vol 17, no 4, pp 311–16.

Shaw, M., Davey Smith, G. and Dorling, D. (2005) 'Health inequalities and New Labour: how the promises compare with real progress', *BMJ*, vol 330, pp 1016–21.

Shaw, M., Lawlor, D.A. and Najman, J.M. (2006) 'Teenage children of teenage mothers: psychological, behavioural and health outcomes from an Australian prospective longitudinal study', *Social Science & Medicine*, vol 62, no 10, pp 2526–39.

Simey, P. and Wellings, K. (2008) 'How do national newspapers report on sex and relationship education in England?' *Sex Education*, vol 8, no 3, pp 357–70.

Simpson, R. (2006) *Delayed childbearing and childlessness in Britain: The 1958 and 1970 cohorts compared*, UTAP Working Paper 2. Edinburgh: Centre for Research on Families and Relationships.

Singh, S. and Darroch, J.E. (2000) 'Adolescent pregnancy and childbearing: levels and trends in developed countries', *Family Planning Perspectives*, vol 31, no 1, pp 14–23.

Singh, S., Darroch, J.E., Frost, J.J. and the Study Team (2001) 'Socioeconomic disadvantage and adolescent women's sexual and reproductive behavior: the case of five developed countries', *Family Planning Perspectives*, vol 33, no 6, pp 251–258 and 289.

Sinha, S., Curtis, K., Jayakody, A., Viner, R. and Roberts, H. (2006) 'Family and peer networks in intimate and sexual relationships amongst teenagers in a multicultural area of East London', *Sociological Research Online*, vol 11, no 1.

Sloggett, A. and Joshi, H. (1998) 'Deprivation indicators as predictors of life events 1981–1992 based on the UK ONS Longitudinal Study', *Journal of Epidemiology & Community Health*, vol 52, no 4, pp 228–33.

Smith, T. (1993) 'Influence of socioeconomic factors on attaining targets for reducing teenage pregnancies', *BMJ*, vol 306, pp 1232–5.

Smith, G.S. and Pell, J.P. (2001) 'Teenage pregnancy and risk of adverse perinatal outcomes associated with first and second births: population based retrospective cohort study', *BMJ*, vol 323, p 476.

SmithBattle, L. (2000) 'Developing a caregiving tradition in opposition to one's past: lessons from a longitudinal study of teenage mothers', *Public Health Nursing*, vol 17, no 2, pp 85–93.

Smithers, R. (1999) 'Minister defends pill for schoolgirls', *Guardian*, 10 May.

Sucoff, C.A. and Upchurch, D.M. (1998) 'Neighborhood context and the risk of childbearing among metropolitan-area black adolescents', *American Sociological Review*, vol 63, no 4, pp 571–85.

Tabberer, S., Hall, C., Prendergast, S. and Webster, A. (2000) *Teenage pregnancy and choice. Abortion or motherhood: influences on the decision*, York, UK: Joseph Rowntree Foundation.

Tan, L.H. and Quinlivan, J.A. (2006) 'Domestic violence, single parenthood, and fathers in the setting of teenage pregnancy', *Journal of Adolescent Health*, vol 38, no 3, pp 201–7.

Teitler, J. (2002) 'Trends in youth sexual initiation and fertility in developed countries: 1960–1995', *The Annals of the American Academy of Political & Social Science*, vol 580, no 1, pp 134–52.

Temmerman, M., Foster, L.B., Hannaford, P., Cattaneo, A., Olsen, J., Bloemenkamp, K.W., Jahn, A. and Silva, M.O. (2006) 'Reproductive health indicators in the European Union: the REPROSTAT project', *European Journal of Obstetrics, Gynecology, and Reproductive Biology*, vol 126, no 1, pp 3–10.

Terry-Humen, E., Manlove, J. and Moore, K.A. (2005) 'Playing catch-up: how children born to teen mothers fare, child trends', Washington DC: National Campaign to Prevent Teen Pregnancy.

The Times (2005) 'Mothers "cover up" depression', 28 November. Available online at: www.timesonline.co.uk/tol/news/uk/health/article597314.ece [accessed 23 October 2008].

Thomson, R. (2000) 'Dream on: the logic of sexual practice', *Journal of Youth Studies*, vol 4, no 4, pp 407–27.

Todman, L.C. (2004) 'Reflections on social exclusion: what is it? How is it different from US conceptualizations of disadvantage? And why Americans might consider integrating it into US social policy discourse', Paper presented to 'City Futures' Conference, Chicago, 8–10 July.

Toynbee, P. (1999) 'Mixed-up teenagers need more than this botched job', *Guardian*, 16 June, p 18.

TPU (Teenage Pregnancy Unit) (2005) *Teenage pregnancy data and analysis toolkit,* London: Teenage Pregnancy Unit

TPU and NRU (Neighbourhood Renewal Unit) (2002) *Teenage pregnancy and neighbourhood renewal: Learning from New Deal for Communities. A pack produced by the Teenage Pregnancy Unit with support from the Neighbourhood Renewal Unit.* London: The Stationery Office.

Unicef (2001) *A league table of teenage births in rich nations*, Innocenti Report Card No 3, Florence: Innocenti Research Centre.

Usher, R. (1999) 'To sir with confusion', *Time Magazine*, vol 154, no 7, 16 August Available online at: www.time.com/time/archive/preview/from_search/0,10987,1107990816–29992,00.html [accessed 07 November 2008].

Usta, I.M., Zoorob, D., Abu-Musa, A., Naassan, G. and Nassar, A.H. (2008) 'Obstetric outcome of teenage pregnancies compared with adult pregnancies', *Acta Obstetricia et Gynecologica Scandinavica*, vol 87, no 2, pp 178–83.

Valois, R.F., Oeltmann, J.E., Waller, J. and Hussey, J.R. (1999) 'Relationship between number of sexual intercourse partners and selected health risk behaviors among public high school adolescents', *Journal of Adolescent Health*, vol 25, no 5, pp 328–35.

van Enk, A. and Gorissen, W.H. (2000) 'Teenage pregnancy and ethnicity in the Netherlands: frequency and obstetric outcome', *European Journal of Contraception and Reproductive Health Care*, vol 5, no 1, pp 77–84.

van Loon, J. (2003) *Deconstructing the Dutch Utopia*, London: Family Education Trust.

Vernon, M.E., Green, J.A. and Frothingham, T.E. (1983) 'Teenage pregnancy: a prospective study of self-esteem and other sociodemographic factors', *Pediatrics*, vol 72, no 5, pp 632–5.

Vinovskis, M.A. (2003) 'Historical perspectives on adolescent pregnancy and education in the United States', *The History of the Family*, vol 8, no 3, pp 399–421.

Wainwright, M. (1999) 'Father in child-mother case faces charges', *Guardian*, 1 September. Accessed online at: http://www.guardian.co.uk/uk/1999/sep/01/martinwainwright1 (accessed: 21/04/09).

Wallace, C. (1987) *For richer, for poorer: Growing up in and out of work*, London, UK: Tavistock.

Wellings, K. and Kane, R. (1999) 'Trends in teenage pregnancy in England and Wales: how can we explain them?', *Journal of the Royal Society of Medicine*, vol 92, no 6, pp 277.

Wellings, K. and Wadsworth, J. (1999) 'Family influences on teenage fertility', in S. McRae (ed), *Changing Britain: Families and households in the 1990s*, Oxford: Oxford University Press, pp 319–33.

Wellings, K., Wadsworth, J., Johnson, A., Field, J. and Macdowall, W. (1999) 'Teenage fertility and life chances', *Reviews of Reproduction*, vol 4, no 3, pp 184–90.

Wellings, K., Wilkinson, P., Grundy, C., Kane, R., Lachowycz, K., Jacklin, P., Stevens, M., Gerressu, M., Parker, R., Stephenson, J., French, R., Kingori, P., Brooker, S., Williams, B., Simpson, C., Larn, P. and British Market Research Bureau (2005) *Teenage pregnancy strategy evaluation: Final report synthesis*, London: Teenage Pregnancy Unit.

Welshman, J. (2002) 'Discourses of poverty: Re-inventing the underclass, 1880–2000', Paper for the Evora Seminar on European Health and Social Welfare Policies, 19–21 September.

West, J. (1999) '(Not) talking about sex: youth, identity and sexuality', *The Sociological Review*, vol 4, no 3, pp 525–47.

Whitehead, E. (2001) 'Teenage pregnancy: on the road to social death', *International Journal of Nursing Studies*, vol 38, no 4, pp 437–46.

Whitehead, E. (2008) 'Exploring relationships in teenage pregnancy', *International Journal of Nursing Practice*, vol 14, no 4, pp 292–5.

Whitley, R. and Kirmayer, L.J. (2008) 'Perceived stigmatisation of young mothers: an exploratory study of psychological and social experience', *Social Science & Medicine*, vol 66, no 2, pp 339–48.

Wiggins, M., Rosato, M., Austerberry, H., Sawtell, M. and Oliver, S. (2005) *Sure Start Plus national evaluation: Final report*, London, UK: Social Science Research Unit, Institute of Education, University of London.

Wilson, H. and Huntington, A. (2006) 'Deviant (M)others: the construction of teenage motherhood in contemporary discourse', *Journal of Social Policy*, vol 35, no 1, pp 59–76.

Wilson, S.H., Brown, T.P. and Richards, R.G. (1992) 'Teenage conception and contraception in the English regions', *Journal of Public Health Medicine*, vol 14, no 1, pp 17–25.

Wintour, P. (1999) 'Blair to stop schools from expelling teenage mothers', *The Observer*, 13 June. Accessed online at: www.guardian.co.uk/uk/1999/jun/13/patrickwintour.theobserver [accessed: 21/04/09].

Wong, J. (1997) 'The "making" of teenage pregnancy', *International Studies in the Philosophy of Science*, vol 11, no 3, pp 273–88.

Young, J. (2007) 'Globalization and social exclusion: the sociology of vindictiveness and the criminology of transgression', in J.M.Hagedorn (ed) *Gangs in the global city: Alternatives to traditional criminology*, Illinois, US: University of Illinois Press, pp 54-96.

Zani, B. (1991) 'Male and female patterns in the discovery of sexuality during adolescence', *Journal of Adolescence*, vol 14, no 2, pp 163–78.

Index

V

Valle, A.-K. 94
Valois, R.F. 31
van Enk, A. 22
van Loon, J. 5, 22, 65
Vernon, M.E. 31
Vinovskis, M.A. 56
Vittanen, T.K. 81

W

Wadsworth, J. 29
Wainwright, M. 61
Wallace, C. 102, 139
welfare benefits 25
Wellings, K. 9, 21, 29, 39, 68, 92, 94,
    97, 99, 132
Welshman, J. 115, 116
West, J. 98
Whitehead, E. 34, 47, 142
Whitley, R. 47
Wiggins, M. 35
Wilson, H. 67, 104, 110
Wilson, S.H. 27
Wolfe, B.L. 81
Wong, J. 3, 56
working class 32, 33, 103–4, 139–40
Worku, S. 82

Y

Young, G. 118
Young, J. 115–16
young fathers 34–5
young marriage 9–10, 101
young motherhood
  advantages 106
  consequences of 75–8, 88–9
    health-related research 75–6, 84–8
    research methodology, difficulties
      76–8
    socioeconomic research 75, 79–84
  disadvantages 106
  intergenerational cycles 29, 30
  as positive experience 104–6, 138,
    140–1
young mothers, peer-education by
    140–1
youth transitions 102

Z

Zani, B. 97

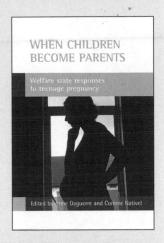